YOU WILL DIE SOMEDAY

By

Seb Rozo

"I'm writing this book because we're all going to die."

+ Jack Kerouac, *Visions of Cody*

"In our early youth we sit before the life that lies ahead of us like children sitting before the curtain in a theatre, in happy and tense anticipation of whatever is going to appear. Luckily we do not know what really will appear."

+ Arthur Schopenhauer, *Essays and Aphorisms*

"In other words, all of my books are lies. They are simply maps of a territory, shadows of a reality, gray symbols dragging their bellies across the dead page, suffocated signs full of muffled sound and faded glory, signifying absolutely nothing. And it is the nothing, the Mystery, the Emptiness alone that needs to be realized: not known but felt, not thought but breathed, not an object but an atmosphere, not a lesson but a life."

+ Ken Wilber, *The Simple Feeling of Being*

PART ONE:

YOU WILL DIE SOMEDAY

"It's only when you're breathing your last that the way you've spent your time will become apparent."

+ Seneca, *Letters From a Stoic,* Letter XXVI

THE INTRODUCTION TO THE CONCLUSION

You will die someday.

I will contradict myself.

And I will disappoint you in some way.

This is all okay and it is all inevitable.

Almost everything, including the very reason you took time out of your Life to read this very book hinges upon something specific:

A curious disappointment of sorts.

When viewed at first glance it seems to be *a curious disappointment* with Life as a general whole perhaps, but yet, when observed with more precision and a sense of honesty, it seems to include a wider range of particulars.

They can be curious disappointments with:

Your friends,

With your family,

With your other half,

With your kid(s),

With your job, with your coworker(s),

With what you own, with what you don't own,

With your lack of purpose, with your sense of purpose,

With your lack of money, with your surplus of money,

With where you live, with where you don't live,

With who you love, with who you don't love,

With your genes, with your DNA,

With your body, with your muscles,

With your height,

With your weight,

With your eyes,

With your ears,

With your nose,

With your lips,

With your hair,

With your skin,

With your penis,

With your vagina, with your breasts, with your ass,

With religion, with mystics,

With theories, with postulates,

With carrot-dangling truths,

With science and its scientists,

With philosophy and its philosophers,

With literature and its writers,

With government,

With politics,

With the president,

With conspiracy theories,

With the mainstream media, with celebrities,

With the environment,

With pollution,

With GMO's, with global agricultural practices,

With the abuse and slaughtering of animals, with the abuse and slaughtering of plants and trees,

With your fears,

With your addictions,

With your guilt,

With your shame,

With your pride,

With your feelings,

With your dreams, with your desires,

With others,

With me,

And, ultimately:

With yourself and your suffering.

This is what it all boils down to:

A curious disappointment with yourself and the world around you.

A sense of wonder and despair in their most refined raiment.

Paradoxically, there is a strange form of relief, with an accompanied burden, once you admit that all of Life is suffering.

That this Life, in its undressed essence, is a strangely complex, yet simple, vacillatory journey that is perpetually bespeckled with fluctuating degrees of seemingly unnecessary pain and rightly deserved pleasure.

With this firmly understood, one's subtle hope for enduring happiness, satisfaction, and things *finally* going your way—which has underlain almost everything in your Life like a finely spun silken fabric—is reluctantly seen in its nakedness and finally put in its place (preferably in a cabinet long-forgotten, located in a basement which just underwent a typhoon).

All of Life is suffering and pleasure.

No one can deny this statement, because no one has never not suffered and/or not felt pleasure.

Suffering and pleasure are innate motifs in the design of our current Matrix.

The world's dynamics are intimately structured in a way to perpetually build you up and tear you down in a nice and rhythmic symphony of uncalled-for surprises and serendipitous delights.

We don't need Buddha's Four Noble Truths, or Schopenhauer's Pessimism, nor Camus' Absurdism, nor any other philosopher-mystic-philosophy to convince us of these truisms; it is crystal clear in our experience, and of those around us.

> "I have no need to dig deeper.
> A single certainty is enough for the seeker.
> He simply has to derive all the consequences from it."
>
> + Albert Camus, *The Myth of Sisyphus*

What *is* needed though are steady reminders, both: of our inevitable suffering, and that of our ineludible death someday.

And it all begins with this generally-specific *curious disappointment* that you now feel radiating within yourself.

It is the beginning of actual intelligence—a form of wisdom if we're even bold enough to proclaim so.

This curious disappointment is the beginning to the end of who you think you are.

Who are you in all actuality?

A mind?

A body?

A soul?

An idea?

An intelligent organization of atoms?

Somethingness?

Nothingness?

Can it ever be fully figured out?

If so, then what?

If not, *then what*?

"All of a sudden, as if a surgical hand of destiny had operated on a long-standing blindness with immediate and sensational results, I lift my gaze from my anonymous life to the clear recognition of how I live. And I see that everything I've done, thought or been is a species of delusion or madness….I look at my past life as at a field lit up by the sun when it breaks through the clouds, and I note with metaphysical astonishment how my most deliberate acts, my clearest ideas and my most logical intentions were after all no more than congenital drunkenness, inherent madness and huge ignorance. I didn't even act anything out. I was the role that got acted. At most, I was the actor's motions."

+ Fernando Pessoa, *The Book of Disquiet*

FRACTAL ONE

You will die someday.

Remind yourself of this truth throughout the entirety of your existence on this planet, or possibly another planet when we finally get to interstellar travel.

Burn this into your mind.

Paint it onto your walls.

Write it down on scattered post-it notes.

Create a daily alert on your phone reminding yourself of your pending non-existence.

You will die someday.

This is the same destiny in which we all share.

Now, considering the entire spectrum of your Life's Experience so far, attempt to remember:

Every single thought that has ever danced through the vastity that is your mind's sweeping expanse.

Attempt to remember:

Every single action that has ever pulsed through your fragile, blood-soaked veins.

Attempt to remember:

Every single word that has ever floated through your beautiful, erogenous lips.

Attempt to remember:

Every single experience that you have willingly and/or unwillingly been a part of without your choosing.

And finally,

Attempt to remember your *every single desire.*

Where do all of these past thoughts, words, actions, desires, and experiences now reside?

Are they to be found anywhere?

If so, how long will they last within the delicate, silky web that is our memory-complex?

How long will they last within the hall of transparent mirrors that is this Contradictory Existence?

Whether it's within a second, an hour, a day, a month, a year, a decade, a century, a millennium, or even, just right now in this moment:

Us and our assemblage of thoughts, words, actions, experiences, and desires are all going to be comfortably buried beneath the Quicksands of Time.

Absolutely everything in our replete History of Consciousness has, will be, and is continuously dissipating within the Fluxing Sands of this Timeless Desert.

Tell me then, with this view in mind, where does our own existence fit into this schema?

Well, when seen through this distinct lens we have managed to inadvertently craft in the previous few pages, our existence now seems to resemble nothing more than mere specks of transitory stardust on the Telescope of Existence.

Nothing more than soft ripples in the Pellucid Lake of Existingness that will, once again, return to stillness.

With sincerity, please answer this truthfully:

What achievement comes from holding water in your hands?

"The clock indicates the moment…

but what does eternity indicate?

Eternity lies in bottomless reservoirs…

its buckets are rising forever and ever,

They pour and they pour and they exhale away."

+ Walt Whitman, "Song of Myself"

FRACTAL TWO

Sirens.

A dog barking.

A paintbrush's bristles moving back and forth on dry wood.

I am currently writing all of this on a wooden desk on the second floor of my house, while my brother is in the next room painting the trims of his bedroom windows pure white.

Let us attempt to deconstruct and qualify all of this in relation to our all-important theme:

You will die someday.

First off: This wooden desk.

Everything contained within it, and on top of it, including: my pens, my pencils, my papers, my rulers, my files, my desk kitsch, and my college degree are all slowly decaying, rotting, and transforming themselves into other forms of matter as we currently speak.

Second off: This house.

Everything contained within it: all of the wood, the brick, the steel, the concrete, the roofing, the walls, the furniture, the appliances, the electronics, all of my notebooks, writings, art, money, plants, and food are all slowly decaying, rotting, rusting, and transforming themselves into other forms of matter as we speak.

Third off: My brother's pure white wooden window trims.

The entirety of the soft wood's physiognomy has already begun rotting and decaying since its initial entrance into Existence, and the newly accompanied pure white paint has already begun chipping and fading the moment it was dexterously slathered on.

And fourth off: My brother and I.

New cells, new thoughts, new moods, and new mutations are repeatedly birthing and dying, birthing and dying, birthing and dying in intelligent metaphysical processes occurring on sub-atomic and trans-sub-atomic planes of Reality incomprehensible to any daring intellect that bravely endeavors to foolishly solve the eternal riddle of Being.

Both of our bodies will someday cease to breathe, be, and/or function and are similarly decaying and transforming into other forms of matter and beyond as we speak.

So, my good friend, I sincerely ask you this then:

What is the reason for all of this stress we harbor within ourselves?

What is the reason for all of this rampant seriousness that pervades and consumes us?

All of this needless running around we do for knowledge and certainty?

All of this muttering and suffering as if we'll be here forever?

We are here for just a mere blink in the eyes of Existence.

And not even a blink, but the thought of a blink.

And even then, we can't pretend to truly know how vast and incomprehensible all of this is.

Therefore, I will mention two of the sincerest statements one can ever claim to know, with absolute certainty, about Existence:

It is.

&

I don't know.

Existence is the one thing we cannot call an illusion.

It *is ising* right now, or else none of this would be happening right now.

And even if we are just living in a simulation, or a supercomputer of sorts, it is still undeniable that *something* is happening in this moment.

But so what?

What now?

What does the knowing of this information change?

Maybe something.

Maybe nothing.

You will still die someday.

Maybe today.

Maybe tomorrow.

Who knows?

Take advantage of the precious time in which you have left.

"Not the fruit of experience, but experience itself is the end. A counted number of pulses only is given to us of a variegated, dramatic life. How may we see in them all that is to be seen in them by the finest senses? How can we pass most swiftly from point to point, and be present always at the focus where the greatest number of vital forces unite in their purest energy?"

+ Walter Pater, *Studies in the History of the Renaissance*

FRACTAL THREE

"Whatsoever is your attitude towards life will be your attitude towards death…"

+ Osho, *This Very Body the Buddha*

You will die someday.

Shock value?

Sure.

But what of it?

The foreboding threat of your impending death will always prickle *something* within you, and for good reason.

A whole range of emotions can immediately make their presence known when the subject comes up:

Fear.

Joy.

Rage.

Relief.

Comfort.

Discomfort.

Gloom.

Doom.

Happiness.

Excitement.

Despair.

No care.

Bliss.

Paranoia.

Illumination.

Liberation.

Now,

Gently direct your Attention on that secluded part of yourself that secretly enjoys, or fears, when I repeat this mantra:

You will die someday.

Why do you derive a secret fear, and/or satisfaction, from hearing this?

Which emotions immediately arise within you?

Don't run away from them. Be here, embrace them.

Hug them with your gentle and understanding Attention.

These emotions are here in your presence to be acknowledged, experienced, and accepted, not dejected.

If needed, endeavor to lightly ponder these reflections:

Why do I feel such fear when attempting to contemplate my inevitable death?

Why do I feel such fear about the Mystery that follows the annihilation of this Mystery?

Why do I feel such fear about my pending, possible, non-existence?

Why do I feel such fear about leaving those who I love and cherish behind?

What am I trying to protect?

Who am I trying to preserve?

FATHER: "Whatever is a reality today, whatever you touch and believe in and that seems real for you today, is going to be—like the reality of yesterday—an illusion tomorrow."

+ Luigi Pirandello, *Six Characters in Search of an Author*

FRACTAL FOUR

"Ikkyu, the Zen master, was very clever even as a boy. His teacher had a precious teacup, a rare antique. Ikkyu happened to break this cup and was greatly perplexed.

Hearing the footsteps of his teacher, he held the pieces of the cup behind him. When the master appeared, Ikkyu asked: 'Why do people have to die?'

'This is natural' explained the older man. 'Everything has to die and has just so long to live.'

Ikkyu, producing the shattered cup, added: 'It was time for your cup to die.'"

+ Paul Reps, *Zen Flesh, Zen Bones*

You will die someday.

What are you afraid to lose?

Your health?

Your wealth?

Your body?

Your house?

Your car?

Your friends?

Your family?

Your mom?

Your dad?

Your brother?

Your sister?

Your husband?

Your wife?

Your boyfriend?

Your girlfriend?

Your daughter?

Your son?

Your pet?

Your job?

Your position?

Your reputation?

Your soul?

What are you so desperately afraid to lose? And why?

In terms of your body:

Are you afraid to lose your capabilities of getting sick? Of contracting diseases? Of feeling pain?

Is your body not slowly decaying in this very moment, on its merry way to the burial grounds?

In terms of your possessions:

Are you afraid to never have that shiny new designer watch ever again?

Does it tell a different kind of time? Cosmic time?

Has it increased your health in some way?

Do you now have a better chance of attracting a partner and engaging in wild monkey sex together?

How about your car?

Will it still fulfill you when teleportation exists?

Will it not rust, wither, and break down someday?

How about your home?

Does sleeping under golden-painted ceilings secure a sweeter sleep?

Do custom silk brocade drapes ensure greater security against thieves?

In terms of loved ones:

Why are you so terribly afraid to lose your friends, your family, your pets, and other loved ones?

Are they ultimately in charge of how you feel and conduct yourself in this Life, and possibly thereafter when you die?

Does anyone or anything truly live forever?

(Yes, of course you're afraid to lose them. Life is precious. You love them dearly. We don't know what comes after this Life. You don't want to imagine their death. You instantaneously grow mentally and physically feeble at the mere mentioning of their passing away. It's unimaginable. To you, it might even be the most foolish exercise the imagination could ever attempt to entertain. Thus, all the more reason to care for your loved ones and enjoy their current existence as profoundly as you can in your remaining time here.)

And finally, in terms of your position, your reputation, your posterity:

Will millions be praising your name, your art, your work years from now? Decades from now? Centuries from now? Millenia?

You probably won't even be here to witness it.

And what's so great about millions praising your name even now?

The masses, as a collective, are superficial, dim-witted, and fickle.

Just look at what they value and praise so highly today.

One day you're an absolute genius, and the next, a complete buffoon.

Another day you're an absolute hero, and the next, a villain.

Think about it, do people's praises actually change the very essence of your being in any way?

> "Does an emerald lose its quality if it is not praised?"
>
> + Marcus Aurelius, *Meditations*

Locate everything and everyone you are so desperately afraid to lose.

Investigate each of them deeply and understand why you're afraid to lose something so transient, so ephemeral in essence.

If this isn't fully grasped and/or understood, you will risk the rest of your Life, especially your final few breaths, in a frenzied scramble, grasping nothing but shadows of your own scattered light.

"Ultimate reality (or Spirit), Ramana [Maharshi] said, cannot be something that pops into consciousness and then pops out. It must be something that is constant, permanent, or, more technically, something that, being *timeless*, is *fully present* at every point in time. Therefore, ultimate reality must also be fully present in deep dreamless sleep, and anything that is *not* present in deep dreamless sleep is *not* ultimate reality."

+ Ken Wilber, *The Essential Ken Wilber*

"The ultimate 'spiritual test,' then, is simply your relation to death....If you want to know the 'ultimate truth' of what you are doing right now, simply submit it to any of those tests. Practicing astrology? If it is not present in deep dreamless sleep, it is not real. Running with wolves? If it is not present a hundred years from now, it is not real....Healing your inner child? If it was not present prior to your parents' birth, it is not real."

+ Ken Wilber, *The Essential Ken Wilber*

FRACTAL FIVE

"Who is prepared to die? Who has lived so fully that they are not threatened by their imaginings of nonexistence?"

+ Stephen Levine, *Who Dies?*

You will die someday.

What do you now do with this reminder?

Do you plunge yourself into a hedonistic, pleasure-seeking, pain-avoiding way of Life?

Do you pummel yourself into a renunciate, an ascetic?

Do you fully open yourself up and seek out a Life full of meaning, joy, ecstasy, and bliss?

Do you retreat yourself into a nihilistic, throwaway attitude about Life?

Do you now want to kill yourself? Do you consider yourself depressed? Do you find yourself feeling sad and melancholic at the most impromptu moments during the day with no justifiable reasons on the horizon to reasonably explain these ephemeral burdens percolating within you?

Have you ever contemplated suicide?

"There is but one truly serious philosophical problem, and that is suicide. Judging whether life is or is not worth living amounts to answering the fundamental question of philosophy. All the rest—whether or not the world has three dimensions, whether the mind has nine or twelve categories—comes afterwards."

+ Albert Camus, *The Myth of Sisyphus*

Why would you want to kill yourself?

Have you reasoned that there is no inherent meaning in the Universe and therefore no point in continuing to live?

Have you reasoned that your suffering, sadness, and pain outweigh your happiness and pleasure, and that there is nothing more that you can possibly take on?

Do you long for some nostalgic sense of home, clarity, and unity in a world that only seems to repeatedly prove otherwise?

Have your stage sets collapsed yet?

"Rising, streetcar, four hours in the office or the factory, meal, streetcar, four hours of work, meal, sleep, and Monday Tuesday Wednesday Thursday Friday and Saturday according to the same rhythm….But one day the 'why' arises…" (Camus).

Have your 'why's' arisen yet?

Why work? Why live? Why die?

Why should I continuously choose to live this perpetual life of absurd suffering punctuated with occasional glimpses of happiness and relief?

Although this topic can be elaborated for pages on end, I will curtail it here.

Looking at suicide from the most objective point of view we will allow ourselves to look at it from—divested of any religious, emotional, and/or societal conditionings—I won't pretend to think that I have found good enough logical reasons to choose or not choose suicide,

And neither can I directly transmit my current sense of purpose and/or meaning of Life to you, but I do rest easy with this understanding in mind, and maybe it will for you as well:

We were given entrance into this Life without any of our conscious approval nor foreknowledge, so why would we expect any different in our exit?

"Through a quarter of my lifetime I was absolutely ignorant of the reasons for everything I saw and heard and felt, and was merely a parrot prompted by other parrots…When I sought to advance along that infinite course, I could neither find one single footpath nor fully discover one single object, and from the upward leap I made to contemplate eternity I fell back into the abyss of ignorance."

+ Voltaire

"If you live well, you will never have to worry about dying.
You can do that even if you have only one day to live.
The question of time is not terribly important;
it is a man-made, artificial concept anyway.

To live well means basically to learn to love."

+ Elisabeth Kübler-Ross,
On Life After Death, "Death Does Not Exist"

FRACTAL SIX

You will die someday.

But, yet, who is this *you* that will die?

Is it:

Your mind?

Your body?

Your soul?

Your Spirit?

Your atoms?

Your Attention? Your Awareness?

What is it?

Any serious answer to this question before death is sheer buffoonery, yet the mere contemplation of it could be considered the apex of our intellectual evolution.

Does anything really die?

What is it that disappears, or seemingly disappears?

If we are nothing but atoms and natural elements, and no soul, do we just cyclically reorganize ourselves back into other material forms of matter?

Or what if we do have souls, do we continue on after death?

Do we continue existing in a divine paradise of heavenly lights, eternal luxuries, and a wonderful reunion of everyone and everything we once loved?

Or what if this whole video game, this simulation, is over altogether?

Do we resume our life as the person in another world who began playing the simulation in the first place, or do we respawn as new characters in another fresh game?

Or what if we do have souls, do we even have the sovereignty to continue onto another life?

Or do we just automatically reintegrate ourselves back into our Source, our Oneness, The Clear White Light, The Ground-And-Goal-Of-All-Being?

Is there any free will in the choosing process?

Well, what if there's no such thing as an individual soul or Oneness?

Is there just eternal blackness after death? Or is there eternal light?

If so, then *who* would be the one witnessing the eternal darkness or light? *Who* would deem it 'eternal?'

So, why all of this worry then?

You will either:

Have your atoms and natural elements reorganized into something else for use in the Universe,

Begin another journey as an individual soul,

Go to a marvelous paradise unimaginable to our to current senses and imagination,

Return to the Original Oneness we all came from,

Restart another simulation,

And/or:

Something else not currently imaginable, intelligible, and/or known that will most likely be taken care of for you nonetheless.

"I ask you, wouldn't you say that anyone who took the view that a lamp was worse off when it was put out than it was before it was lit was an utter idiot?"

+ Seneca, *Letters From a Stoic*, Letter LIV

FRACTAL SEVEN

You will die someday.

Are your days wasteful?

Or are they purposeful?

Do you take advantage of all the precious time in which you have left?

Or do you fill it with mindless distractions and profligate minutiae?

What is actually meaningful for you?

Are you conscious of the levels of meaning you give to each person, thing, and/or situation?

Are you conscious of the levels of meaning you give to each thought, feeling, sensation, and/or emotion that arises within you?

What do you want to accomplish before you die?

What do you want to cross off your bucket list?

Why are those specific things even on your bucket list to begin with? Are they truly worth pursuing?

Revise them carefully.

Rid yourself of any unnecessary trifles and trivialities that loom in yourself and in your environs.

What do you truly want to pursue in this Lifetime?

Money?

Fame?

Glory?

Love?

Lust?

Art?

A skill?

A sport?

A craft?

Beauty?

Justice?

Injustice?

Religion?

Enlightenment?

Marriage?

Kids?

No kids?

What do you truly want to pursue in this Finite Play of Lights?

"All of this is dream and phantasmagoria, and it matters little whether the dream be of ledger entries or of well-crafted prose. Does dreaming of princesses serve a better purpose than dreaming of the front door to the office?"

+ Fernando Pessoa, *The Book of Disquiet*

FRACTAL EIGHT

You will die someday.

This could be your first life.

This could be your last life.

This could be your 7,343,239th life.

Does it matter either way?

What are you going to do with all the knowledge you have amassed in this Lifetime so far?

All of that information you have ingested?

All of those books you have read?

All of those videos and entertainments you have absorbed?

All of those innumerable hours staring at a screen?

Has any of it increased the quality of your Life in some way?

Has any of it made you a better person in some way?

What are you going to do with all those seemingly profound realizations of Life and creative insights that you've intuited over the years?

You could die tomorrow and it could all be lost.

You had all of this knowledge, all of this creativity energy to share with the world, and you squandered it.

You selfishly hoarded all of those valuable experiences, all of those creative imaginings, all to yourself.

You wasted away all those pearls of imagination which could have potentially transformed another person's Life for the better.

To keep your cozy little existence safe—and the reputation with those around you intact—you compromised the agreement you made with Life.

Life whispered her secrets to you, to lovingly share with others, to connect with others, but no, you chose to hoard it all to yourself—or even worse, you chose not to even act on them.

There is too much of little time left.

Share what you feel the truest expression of yourself to be.

Share what you feel the truest expression of Reality to be.

You will die someday.

"The highest virtue one can exercise is to accept the responsibility of discovering and transmitting the whole truth."

+ Lao Tzu, *Hua Hu Ching*

FRACTAL NINE

"Equally good is the answer given by the person, whoever it was (his identity is uncertain), who when asked what was the object of all the trouble he took over a piece of craftsmanship when it would never reach more than very few people replied:

'A few is enough for me; so is one; and so is none.'"

+ Seneca, *Letters From a Stoic*, Letter VII

You will die someday.

Have you studied what you *truly* wanted to study?

Have you created what you *truly* wanted to create?

Have you written that book yet?

That novel?

That memoir?

That play?

That screenplay?

That short story?

That autobiography?

That philosophical masterpiece?

What about that painting?

That landscape?

That self-portrait?

That still life?

That fresco?

What about that film?

That short film?

That feature film?

That TV show?

That documentary?

How about that musical composition?

That album?

That mix?

That symphony?

That concerto?

That opera?

That film score?

How about that business idea?

That restaurant?

That online store?

That product?

That service?

What are you waiting for?

Are these ideas of creation not alive within you in this very moment?

Are they not living somewhere in the riverbanks of your memory stream?

Create!

DIRECTOR: We have enough analyses,
Now I am eager to see deeds;
While you exchange your pleasantries,
Another's useful plan succeeds.
Your talk of moods kindles no flame,
The waverer always waits and loses;
If you are poets as you claim,
Then prove that you command the muses.
You know just what we need, I think:
We want a potent brew to drink.
Concoct it now without delay!
Tomorrow we still miss what is not done today;
There is no day that one should skip,
But one should seize without distrust
The possible with iron grip;
Once grasped, one will not let it slip,
But one works on because one must.

+ Johann Wolfgang von Goethe, *Faust*

"Brahms once remarked that the mark of an artist is how much he throws away. Nature, the great creator, is always throwing things away. A frog lays several million eggs at a sitting. Only a few dozen of these become tadpoles, and only a few of those become frogs. We can let imagination and practice be as profligate as nature."

+ Stephen Nachmanovitch, *Free Play*

FRACTAL TEN

You will die someday.

Are you at least enjoying your allotted time here on Earth?

How do you spend your time?

Do you do things that are forced upon you?

Or do you do things out of your own volition?

Do you do things that give you purpose? Things that are meaningful to you?

Or do you do things without thought, without conscious intention?

What do you spend your priceless time on Earth doing?

Do you do things that remind you that time seemingly exists?

Or do you do things that remind you that time doesn't exist?

You　　　Will　　　Die　　　Someday.

Why do you suffocate your days with nonsense and claptrap?

This could be your last day, your last minute, your last hour!

Why waste it on stress? Anger? Panic? Anxiety?

Why not invest it in more fruitful and enjoyable ways of being?

Why do you believe that it is *you* who is actually stressed?

Why do you believe that it is *you* who is actually angry?

Why do you believe that it is *you* who is actually in panic?

Why do you believe that it is *you* who is actually anxious?

What reality do these feelings and emotions contain other than their temporariness and our crude interpretations of them?

INEZ: And yet, just look at me, see how weak I am, a mere breath on the air, a gaze observing you, a formless thought that thinks you.

+ Jean-Paul Sartre, *No Exit*

You will die someday.

Your body will cease to body.

Your breath will cease to breathe.

And your mind will cease to mind.

Your body will return to the Universe's Earth.

You breath will return to the Universe's Winds.

And your mind will return to the Universe's Memory Bank.

So, what is with all this fussing and hubbub about our inevitable death?

Does a rose make any fuss about its natural fate?

It begins as a seed, matures into its utmost climax, and begins its descent back down from where it came from.

Do we not also begin as a seed, mature into our utmost climax, and begin our descent back down from where we came from?

Why do we wish to go against Nature and its natural processes?

We will all die someday.

"Can't you see how fortunate you are? You have worn yourself out through ceaseless striving, you have filled your muscles with pain and anguish. And what have you achieved but to bring yourself one day nearer to the end of your days?"

+ *Gilgamesh*

FRACTAL ELEVEN

"Every moment of our life belongs to the present only for a moment; then it belongs for ever to the past. Every evening we are poorer by a day. We would perhaps grow frantic at the sight of this ebbing away of our short span of time were we not secretly conscious in the profoundest depths of our being that we share in the inexhaustible well of eternity, out of which we can for ever draw new life and renewed time.

You could, to be sure, base on considerations of this kind a theory that the greatest *wisdom* consists in enjoying the present and making this enjoyment the goal of life, because the present is all that is real and everything else merely imaginary. But you could just as well call this mode of life the greatest *folly*: for that which in a moment ceases to exist, which vanishes as completely as a dream, cannot be worth any serious effort."

+ Arthur Schopenhauer, "On the Vanity of Existence"

You will die someday.

This very moment is it.

This is all you have, and all you ever will have throughout the entirety of your existence here:

Just this moment, and the next one after that.

So please, take this moment.

Feel it. Enjoy it. Extract its generous immediacy.

Okay, so now that that previous moment has evaporated, and a new one has replaced it we can comfortably ask each other:

Where did that moment go?

Where is it to be found now?

In our fluxing memory of memories?

The same exact phenomenon applies to us in the entire History of Consciousness.

1,000,000 and 1 years will pass from now. Where do you see yourself and the memory of your Life lived in those parameters of time?

Who will actually remember that you existed once? Who will remember what you felt? How you felt? What you created? What you thought? How you thought? And why would those things even matter?

You are *here, right now.*

Not 1,000,000 and 1 years from now.

Do what needs to be done in this Lifetime, now, as you think best.

* * *

You will die someday.

Do you want to know when?

Do you *actually* want to know the exact date and time you will die in?

What would be the advantage of knowing when? What would you do with this information?

Would you begin to anxiously count the days, hours, and seconds until that fateful day?

Or would you begin to live more intensely, making each moment count, and doing what needs to be done?

Would you make yourself a victim and curse your existence and everything you have left of it?

Or would you make yourself entirely responsible for everything that happens within the purview and control of what you have left before you?

What if we solved immortality and could live forever?

Would you even want to?

What would happen to our conceptions of God, faith, society, and religion if we solved the enigma of our mortality?

Do you not feel as if this Life is only a fleeting dream that ceaselessly strives to convince you that it is real?

Do you not feel this Amorphous Fleetingness in everything that you come into contact with?

Your thoughts, fleeting.

Your senses, fleeting.

Your actions, fleeting.

Your spoken words, fleeting.

The people around you, fleeting.

The situations around you, fleeting.

Your feelings, fleeting.

And your personality, fleeting.

Thoughts arise in our experience, and then they dissolve right after.

Where did they go?

Sensations arise in our experience, and then dissolve right after.

Where did they go?

Actions, from ourselves and others, arise in our experience and dissolve right after.

Where did they go?

Spoken words, from ourselves and others, arise in our experience and then dissolve right after.

Where did they go?

The people we meet arise in our experience, and then dissolve right after.

Where did they go?

Situations arise in our experience, and then dissolve right after.

Where did they go?

Feelings arise in our experience, and then dissolve right after.

Where did they go?

And finally, your personality arises—which comprises your physical, mental, and emotional experience—and then dissolves right after.

Where did it come from?

And where did it go?

If you don't feel that this Life resembles a dream, then how about a movie?

A movie in which you play your role while simultaneously going through your own Hero's Journey.

A movie with its ups and down,

Its scenes and settings,

Its friends and foes,

Its antagonists and protagonists,

Its motifs and themes,

Its births and its deaths,

Its loves and hates,

Its good and evil.

Do you not feel as if you are nothing more than a mere projection of purpose and activity?

A sentient ray of seemingly solid light that pretends to project a transient character onto the Movie Screen of Life?

And not only a projection, but do you not feel as if *you are also* the Movie Screen of Life, on which every sentient ray of seemingly solid light is playfully shining on?

A Movie Screen whose essence is never modified by what is projected on it?

A Movie Screen continuously projecting Itself back into Itself?

"However much the plays and the masks on the world's stage may change it is always the same actors who appear. We sit together and talk and grow excited, and our eyes glitter and our voices grow shriller: just so did *others* sit and talk a thousand years ago: it was the same thing, and it was the *same people*: and it will be just so a thousand years hence. The contrivance which prevents us from perceiving this is *time*."

+Arthur Schopenhauer, *Essays and Aphorisms*

"The entire life of the human soul is mere motions in the shadows. We live in a twilight of consciousness, never in accord with whom we are or think we are….We're something that goes on during the show's intermissions; sometimes, through certain doors, we catch a glimpse of what may be no more than scenery.

The world is one big confusion, like voices in the night."

+ Fernando Pessoa, *The Book of Disquiet*

FRACTAL TWELVE

"The ephemeral generations of man are born and pass away in quick succession; individual men, burdened with fear, want and sorrow, dance into the arms of death. As they do so they never weary of asking what it is that ails them and what the whole tragi-comedy is supposed to mean. They call on Heaven for an answer, but Heaven stays silent. Instead of a voice from Heaven there come along priests with revelations."

+ Arthur Schopenhauer, "On Religion"

You will die someday.

Maybe, more accurately said:

Your experience of Life will come to a close at some point.

Why do you think a heaven exists?

Why do you think a hell exists?

Why do you think an afterlife exists?

Why do you think eternity exists?

Why do you think a nothingness exists?

Why do you think that a Higher Intelligence exists?

Who or what do you believe in?

God?

Jesus?

Yahweh?

Allah?

Muhammad?

Brahman?

Vishnu?

Shiva?

Satan?

Jah?

Waheguru?

Animal spirits?

Aliens?

Greek gods?

Psychoactive substances?

Atoms?

Fire?

Water?

Wind?

Gaia?

Buddha?

Nothingness?

Emptiness?

Reason?

Science?

The Tao?

The Universe?

Oneness?

The Sound of One Hand Clapping?

What is that thing, that god, that belief system, that concept, that poetic metaphor for a Higher Intelligence in which you put all of your metaphysical eggs in?

Ask yourself:

Do I fear death?

Well, of course you do.

We all do.

But, why do you fear it to the extent that you presently do?

Why such shaky faith in your god, in your concept, in your poetic metaphor for a Higher Intelligence?

Strive to find *that* which is always constant in your experience of Life and use it as your unfailing foundation.

You will know when you have found it.

"In man's life his time is a mere instant, his existence a flux, his perception fogged, his whole bodily composition rotting, his mind a whirligig, his fortune unpredictable, his fame unclear. To put it shortly: all things of the body stream away like a river, all things of the mind are dreams and delusion; life is warfare, and a visit in a strange land; the only lasting fame is oblivion."

+ Marcus Aurelius, *Meditations*

CONCLUDING INTRODUCTIONS

If the premise is accepted that we are all made out of the same *Essential Vibratingness*, devoid of any conceptions attached to it such as: good or evil, sacred or profane, heavenly or hellish, eternal or infinite, ordinary or extraordinary, etc,

Then why do we believe there is something independent of this *Essential Vibratingness*?

Why do we believe that there is *something else* that is able to harm, alter, and/or modify who we are: this *Essential Vibratingness*.

Why do we believe that the situations and environments we find ourselves in are inherently different and independent from our *Essential Vibratingness*?

Why do we believe that the people we find ourselves interacting with each day are different and independent from our *Essential Vibratingness*?

Aren't they composed of the very same *Essential Vibratingness* that composes our minds, our chemistry, and the very fabric of our Reality?

What makes you think that there is anything separate or external between the situation in front of you and your *Essential Vibratingness*?

Aren't they both being simultaneously experienced within you?

They are cohabiting the same immediate experience in this very instant.

And even saying "cohabiting" implies twoness.

They were one to begin with, and they are one to end with.

It is we ourselves through thoughts and their resultant perceptions that have separated the two and believed it and carried it through time.

Who told us to do this?

* * *

It seems as if one of the biggest hindrances to one's inescapable self-realization (if it even exists) is the admitting to oneself that there are actually no "other people."

No "others" that truly exist. Not even yourself.

This very admittance, this very realization, would shatter the perception of your Reality.

And to further elaborate on this potentially horrifying, or liberating notion, I am reminded how in dreams people and situations seem to take on a personality and gravity of their own—a convincing sentience of sorts.

That is…until I wake up.

And a luminous clarity reveals to me that all of it was only a dream.

Each person, each thing, each situation in the dream—including my sense of self—seemed to be only an idea, a figment, a creation of the imagination's whim.

So, with all of this, I, sincerely, and honestly, ask myself, and you, the question:

Could this also be…

THRASYMACHUS: Well, I wouldn't give twopence for your immortality if it doesn't include the continued existence of my individuality.

PHILALETHES: But perhaps you would be willing to bargain a little. Suppose I guarantee you the continued existence of your individuality, but on condition it is preceded by a completely unconscious death-sleep of three months.

THRASYMACHUS: I would agree to that.

PHILALETHES: But since when we are completely unconscious we have no notion of the passage of time, it is all one to us whether, while we are lying in that death-sleep, three months or ten thousand years pass in the conscious world. For in either case, when we awake we have to take on trust how long we have been sleeping. So that it will be all the same to you whether your individuality is restored to you after three months or ten thousand years.

THRASYMACHUS: That cannot very well be denied.

PHILALETHES: But now, if after these ten thousand years have passed it was forgotten to wake you up, this would not, I think, be a very great misfortune, since your period of non-being would have been so long compared with your brief period of being you would have got quite used to it. What is certain, however, is that you would not have the least idea you had failed to be woken up. And you would be completely content with the whole thing if you knew that the mysterious mechanism which moves your present phenomenal form had not ceased for one moment throughout these ten thousand years to produce and move other phenomena of the same sort.

THRASYMACHUS: No, you can't cheat me out of my individuality in that way. I have stipulated that my individuality should continue to exist, and I cannot be reconciled to its loss by mechanisms and phenomena. I, I, I want to exist! *that* is what I want, and not an existence I first have to be argued into believing I possess.

PHILALETHES: But just look around you! That which cries 'I, I, I want to exist' is not you alone; it is everything, absolutely everything…

   + Arthur Schopenhauer, "The Indestructibility of Being"

"Just as one sun is reflected in numerous puddles, each showing a separate image of the same sun, so the unlimited and ever-present light of pure Knowing is reflected in seven billion minds as the feeling 'I am,' giving rise to the appearance of seven billion selves."

+ Rupert Spira

You will die someday.

PART DEUX:

ESSAYS AND APHORISMS

ONE PREREQUISITE

1.   Reality always has one prerequisite in order to exist:

It has to be right here.

"To be entirely free, and at the same time entirely dominated by law, is the eternal paradox of human life that we realise at every moment."

+ Oscar Wilde, *De Profundis*

EVERYTHING THAT YOU THINK YOU KNOW IS SKEWED

2. Everything,

   Absolutely everything that *you think you know*,

   Is skewed.

   Absolutely everything.

   Now, let that gently sink in.

   But actually let it sink in.

   Don't just look for the next sentence after this one to distract yourself like you do with every other book you read.

   You know what? Better yet, go and take a lap.

   Reread the top again and make your way back here. I'll wait.

Are you aware that even the previous claim that:

"Everything that you think you know is skewed" is equally skewed as well?

And even *that* statement as well.

So, where is The Truth to be found then?

And why is it even called the the Truth?

Doesn't that concomitantly imply that Non-Truth exists somewhere?

We say we need to "find The Truth,"

We say we need to "be The Truth."

But yet, *who* is this *who* who needs find and be this intangible ideal?

Why do we automatically imply that a single drop of Non-Truth exists somewhere?

Isn't it All One as the wisest sages through history have calmly tried to tell us, but yet, have failed to reasonably explain the obvious plurality that perpetually engulfs us?

We must question everything.

Even questioning the very need to question everything.

We are right here, right now, together, transcending time through time.

This is undeniable.

We (whatever *we* might mean) begin this Life by being dropped into a specific galaxy, which includes a specific solar system, planet, region of the planet, mind, body, and a family.

This occurs without any of our conscious choosing and we are now forced to accept and entertain it all somehow.

So, what now?

What are we to do?

There is no certified Life Instruction Manual ready to answer questions such as:

What is all of this?

Where did we come from?

Where are we going after?

Who am I?

Why do things exist rather than not existing at all?

What's inherently *good*? What's inherently *bad*?

Are morals and ethics objective, or are they subjective and merely fodder for endless interpretation?

How are we supposed to move on this terrestrial landscape as purposefully and as pleasurably as we possibly can?

What is my purpose?

Is there even such a thing? Or is it a label we have concocted out of the structure of our invented language to paste onto the intangible uselessness, boredom, and inertia we feel as human beings from time to time?

Or if purpose does exist, does 1 over-arching purpose exist for us all, or do I as an individual have to create multiple iterations of it for myself on a continuous basis?

Is anything at all meaningful if we're all just hurtling speedily towards our death someday?

And finally:

Who or *what* is this strange babbling voice that has been placed in the center of my head, endlessly narrating everything within me uselessly, day after day, moment after moment?

How can I reasonably admit that free will exists if the next thoughts and impulses that enter my mind are not of my own doing?

"Imagine that you have spent your whole life living in a large house, serving a demanding old man who lives in a room on the top floor.

Although you never see the man, you spend from morning till night doing his chores. One evening, during a rare break, you are lamenting your fate to a friend. The friend suggests that you reason with the old man.

When he hears that you never see him, let alone speak to him, he is puzzled and encourages you to go and find him.

Your are reluctant to begin with, but after several such encounters with your friend, you venture into the old man's room.

On your first visit you only have the courage to peep round the door, but you cannot see the man. When you report this to your friend he encourages you to be bolder and have a good look into the room.

You make more visits to the old man's room, and each time you search his quarters a little more thoroughly. It is only after several visits that you are convinced that there is no old man….

As we look more and more deeply into the nature of ourself we find that there is no entity there. We spend our lives serving a non-existent entity. It is only our imagination that binds us, and it is clarity that liberates."

+ Rupert Spira, *The Transparency of Things*

THE DIALECTIC OF SIMULTANEOUSLY BEING A SOMEONE & A NO ONE

3. It is truly beyond any form of questioning that:

   We are aware of something happening in this very moment.

   But the next question that naturally arises after admitting this is:

   Who or *what* is it that is experiencing this 'something happening in this very moment?'

   And to even begin properly investigating this question, we must plunge into it from another angle.

   We as human beings, for a long time now, have had trouble reconciling and making sense of a certain dynamic:

   The dynamic between being a someone and a no one.

   A doer vs. a non-doer.

   Free will vs. no will.

   The Bewildering Perplexity is this:

   On one hand, we are gifted Awareness: the ability of knowing that things and your sense of being are happening and existing right now at all.

Awareness has no form, nor tangible characteristics.

It is how we experience and are aware of absolutely everything that happens in our Life.

Awareness is *that* in which all experience arises and is known by, and it is also *that* in which all experience is made of.

And on the other hand, we have a body.

Which *does* have form, and tangible characteristics.

Our body is our means of transportation in this Life.

It is *that* in which Awareness makes itself present and known.

Thus, the subsequent question is this:

Who is the one who is aware of its own Awareness?

Most will instantly answer:

"Me! Who else?"

A logical answer of course.

Who else would be experiencing this moment right now?

Yet, few venture far enough to appropriately question *who* this *me* actually is.

Is there in actuality a permanent, stable *me* or is there just the moving and perpetually changing illusion of one?

If answered and investigated honestly, a crucial imperative will begin to dawn upon one to find out what is actually true for them in their own experience.

What we can claim with confidence about Life and our individual and collective experience of it is this:

Awareness is right here, right now.

Fantastic. Wonderful. Great.

What else can we hope to get away with saying?

We can never fully grasp our own Awareness physically nor find its exact location anywhere.

All that we know is that it is *here, now,* wherever this *here, now* might be.

Therefore, if we were to give our best guesstimate as to where our Awareness lives, we would obviously say our bodies.

Our body is the vehicle that allows us to experience this wonderfully confusing planet with its array of attendant emotions, feelings, sensations, perceptions, pains, pleasures, desires, and experiences of all sorts.

That being so, let us reiterate the earlier questions:

How are we able to experience Life?

Awareness: the simple ability of recognizing that *something* is, in fact, happening right now, at all.

And, where does this Awareness *seem* to emanate from and reside in?

Our body.

Thus, the Grand Paradox is born:

Awareness, the formlessly evanescent activity that is present and happening in every human being, the thing that allows us to recognize that experience is happening right now resides in:

The body, a physically tangible organism where we can specifically pinpoint where and how processes are happening and coming from.

Thus, in this Delightful Paradox of the merging between the formless (Awareness) and the form (the body), an identity is inevitably formed.

On one hand, we are seemingly someone.

And on the other, we are seemingly no one.

"Simply ask, Who am I? Who am I? Who am I?

I am aware of my feelings, so I am not my feelings—Who am I? I am aware of my thoughts, so I am not my thoughts—Who am I? Clouds float by in the sky, thoughts float by in the mind, feelings float by in the body—and I am none of those because I can Witness them all.

Moreover, I can doubt that clouds exist, I can doubt that feelings exist, I can doubt that objects of thought exist—but I cannot doubt the Witness exists in this moment, because the Witness would still be there to witness the doubt.

I am not objects in nature, not feelings in the body, not thoughts in the mind, for I can Witness them all. I am that Witness—a vast, spacious, clear, pure, transparent Openness that impartially notices all that arises, as a mirror spontaneously reflects all its objects…"

+ Ken Wilber, *The Simple Feeling of Being*

CURIOSITY ALWAYS SEEKS TO EXTINGUISH ITSELF

"Each of us has an image of what we think we are or what we should be, and that image, that picture, entirely prevents us from seeing ourselves as we actually are."

+ Jiddu Krishnamurti, *Freedom From the Known*

4. *You* are *you*.

You are no one else but *you*.

You are a never-before-seen-character—employed from a universal casting agency—that has never existed before and will, perhaps, never exist again.

You are free to be *you* and everything that entails and transcends this water-like, wave-like, ever-in-flux-*you*.

Do away with everything of little importance that this current-you *thinks* that it has to do.

Who's telling *you* what to do?

Do away with everything of little importance that this current-you *thinks* it has to be.

Who's telling *you* what to be?

Do away with everything of little importance that this current-you *thinks* it has to think.

Who's telling *you* what to think?

* * *

All we're really doing in this Life is perpetually celebrating and expressing a Multitudinously Singular, Obvious-But-Not-So-Obvious, Palpably Amorphous Shining Energy.

And thus, with this premise in play, and now aiming our sights into both the spheres of Art and identity, it seems justified in assuming that an artist's primary responsibility is to consistently point out and express this Energy, while using rejuvenating combinations of ideas, images, and insights that have never been juxtaposed before, while simultaneously integrating one's own idiosyncratic flair, imagination, and unequaled Life experience as unrelenting fodder for creation.

One must always keep fresh in the mind that absolutely everything you do reveals you.

And in any work of Art that you create, there will always be that which you meant to include, and that which you didn't mean to include.

Your Life and your Art always travel in unison.

"When I hear people speak of the evolution of an artist, it seems to me that they are considering him standing between two mirrors that face each other and reproduce his image an infinite number of times, and that they contemplate the successive images of one mirror as his past, and the images of the other mirror as his future, while his real image is taken as his present. They do not consider that they are all the same images in different planes."

+ Pablo Picasso, *Picasso: In His Words*

SCENE AFTER SCENE

"Life is the farce we are all forced to endure."

+ Arthur Rimbaud, "A Season In Hell"

5. While living, the stories of others will naturally play themselves out all around you, in the form of scenes and situations overlapping with your own current story.

   With or without your consent, this will inevitably happen.

   With this, one's continuous job is to:

   1. Acknowledge and accept these scenes and stories playing out in front of you with the least amount of judgement.

   2. Find the informational essence you need to extract from the current story the scene is providing.

   3. Figuring out what your role is within the scene, who it is that you need to talk to, and what it is that you need to say and/or do.

   And:

   4. Appreciating the scene, the associated story, and people for existing and happening at all.

Whatever the scene might be, whatever the story might look like, they are there—in front of you—happening within your immediate being.

Yes, every scene happens within you:

A scene supplies thoughts that arise within you.

A scene supplies visuals that illumine within you.

A scene supplies smells that effervesce within you.

A scene supplies feelings and sensations that burst within you.

And a scene also supplies sounds that echo within you.

All of this naturally brings forth the questions:

To whom is this phenomena occurring to?

Whom is the whom experiencing what exactly?

While I suspect that there can never be a definitive answer to this quandary, one of my favorite contemplations comes from our contemporary American philosopher, Ken Wilber, who points out what another American philosopher, William James has once pointed out:

"Now you cannot hear the hearer for a simple reason. As William James pointed out, you cannot hear the hearer because the hearer is nothing but the entire stream of sounds heard."

Okay, so what?

What does one do with this obscure information?

Well, one can continue on doing what many of our ancestors have done for years now:

Identifying ourselves—our personality—our sense of who we think we are— with the scene and various phenomena playing out in front of and within us.

And this means:

Investing our thoughts, feelings, sensations, and our overall sense of being "a someone" with the current scene, the current situation.

Essentially, you take on whichever creative scene—this current moment's happenings—as an extension of who you think you are.

You think this scene defines you as a person in some way, and you begin investing your energy into it.

You then attempt to direct the scene—both mentally and physically—in a way that you feel more accurately defines who you think you are and how you want to it be.

For example, a scene can conjure up feelings of embarrassment within you.

So, now, because you are identifying this current moment and its happenings with *who you think you are*, you feel embarrassed by extension, and now you have to do your best within the scene to direct it to a conclusion that you think more accurately portrays "you," which doesn't include this imaginary embarrassment anymore.

We all do this to varying degrees with a plethora of different thoughts, sensations, feelings and such ceaselessly directing our sails.

But now knowing that this phenomenon occurs scene after scene throughout our Lives, one begins ruminating on how to ditch this perception and substitute it with a fresher one—one that deals with a freer way of living and perceiving things.

And so, we arrive at the recurring paradox of perceptions we encounter at every turn in this Dialectical Game of Life:

"Something becomes an other: this other is itself somewhat: therefore it likewise becomes an other, and so on *ad infinitum*."

+ Hegel, *Encyclopedia of the Philosophical Sciences*

With this system of reasoning, it then seems logical to admit that our ability to substitute perceptions for other perceptions inadvertently acquires the flavor of being both a blessing and a curse.

It feels as if we are are swapping red-tinted glass for yellow-tinted ones, with the fastidious hope of seeing more clearly.

"So, what is one to do after all?"

Investigate the nature of the self that you think you are.

Investigate the beliefs and perceptions that this self holds about itself, its world, and about others.

And finally, find the beliefs and perceptions that allow you to live the freest life imaginable.

"Everything, for us, is in our concept of the world. To modify our concept of the world is to modify the world for us, or simply to modify the world, since it will never be, for us, anything but what it is for us. That inner inner justice we summon to write a fluent and beautiful page, that true reformation of enlivening our dead sensibility—these things are the truth, our truth, the only truth. Everything else in the world is scenery, picture frames for our feelings, book bindings for our thoughts."

+ Fernando Pessoa, *The Book of Disquiet*

"We've all had the experience of looking through a window and suddenly noticing our own reflection in the glass. At that moment we have a choice: to use the window and see the world beyond, or to use it as a mirror. It is extraordinarily easy to shift back and forth between these two views but impossible to truly focus on both simultaneously. This shift offers a very good analogy both for what it is like to recognize the illusoriness of the self for the first time and for why it can take so long to do it."

+ Sam Harris, *Waking Up*

THINK OF YOURSELF AS A MOVING WHEEL

"But since the uttermost limit of Being is ended and perfect,

Then it is like to the bulk of a sphere well-rounded on all sides,

Everywhere distant alike from the centre; for never there can be anything greater or anything less, on this side or that side."

+ Parmenides, *On Nature*

6. Think of yourself as a moving wheel.

The tire and the spokes are your periphery.

And the hub is your center.

Now, imagine a normal day.

What happens to you during the course of a normal day?

Thoughts.

Thoughts that ceaselessly arise within your mind's stratosphere —without your conscious doing or willing—giving you the continuous illusion that *you* are these thoughts, and thus leading you to derive your sense of identity through them.

For example:

If an anxious thought arises in your Attention, you now believe *yourself* to be anxious.

If an angry thought arises in your Attention, you now believe *yourself* to be angry.

And so on.

Hence, following our make-shift model of the moving wheel, we can say this:

Thoughts go round and round our periphery—which is the tire in this case.

Round and round and round all day.

And after a while, you, the whole wheel, begins to forget that there is a hub, a center that holds everything together.

And you, the whole wheel, begin believing that you are only the tire—these thoughts—and nothing else.

But, once you begin to remember and have glimpses of the center—the place that holds everything together without doing anything, which has been here the entire time—you begin to feel that there is *something more* than just the periphery.

You begin to feel that there is *something more* than just thoughts to define who you are and how you feel on a day-to-day basis.

You begin to feel that there is *something more* balanced in play to define the nature of your identity and how it perpetually expresses itself.

This hub—our center— is a *formlessly inexhaustible, location-less space we always and only are in which all of experience arises.*

It is a simple recognition that your very nature is utterly free and immeasurable space.

You are not your thoughts, nor are you a permanent nor solid entity.

Your essential nature is *this very space* in which these very thoughts and energies are making themselves apparent *in this very moment.*

This is an exquisitely ornate and sentient space that we all as human beings endlessly bathe in because it is all we ever know, and are.

There are no comparisons to this space because the very fabric of our Existence, the very fabric of each and every one of our experiences in this Life is only made out of this exquisitely intelligent space.

Unfortunately though, this space is so painfully obvious that it is habitually overlooked and suppressed by our perceptions and prejudices of what we think, what we think others think, what we feel, what we feel others feel, and what we've been conditioned to believe Reality really is.

Connecting this to the previous Sam Harris quote about the window, it seems we can choose two clear options here:

We can either choose to use the window as a mirror to bounce back our thoughts and ideas of what we think, and have been told Reality is.

Or,

We can use the window to look through and realize that this world and our essential nature is nothing else but free and unrestrained space.

* * *

Can you locate the permanent entity that you think yourself to be in this moment?

Can you pinpoint its exact longitude and latitude?

Can you measure its every contour and outline?

Can you find any vestige of permanency in its identity?

Can you find any permanency in its concepts about Life?

Can you feel this immediate space within and around us right now?

Can you feel everything arising in this moment: sounds, smells, sensations, thoughts, visuals, and emotions, is only because of this space that you, I, and everything else in Existence innately and obviously share together?

Fundamentally, space is our our Intrinsic Nature and our Inalienable Birthright.

And even if it's just for a couple mere moments in time,

> *Receiving a taste of your own center,*
>
> *Changes the perception of yourself,*
>
> *And the world around you,*
>
> *Forever.*

"Thirty spokes converge upon a single hub;
It is on the hole in the center that the use of the cart hinges.

We make a vessel from a lump of clay;
It is the empty space within the vessel that makes it useful.

We make doors and windows for a room;
But it is these empty spaces that make the room livable.

Thus, while the tangible has advantages,
It is the intangible that makes it useful."

+ Lao Tzu, *Tao Teh Ching*

GLIMPSES OF THE MACROCOSM

> "Admitting that the world has no meaning simultaneously implies that it has meaning."
>
> + Valvudo Ariapeggi

7. It only takes one infinitesimally minute glimpse of the Macrocosm to put your previously believed and remarkably self-centered perceptions of Life into their place and be replaced with pristine perceptions of *immediate meaning and purpose without belief.*

Whether it's a feeling, a word, a sensation, an observation, a conversation, a piece of art, or even nothing but a joyful nothing in the most impromptu instance,

Our Life is meaningful beyond any form of belief.

And without a replete and profound acceptance of Life, there is nothing worth truly living for.

"The fact that the universe is illuminated where you stand—that your thoughts and moods and sensations have a qualitative character in this moment—is a mystery, exceeded only by the mystery that there should be something rather than nothing in the first place."

+ Sam Harris, *Waking Up*

SCATTERED REFLECTIONS ON SOME OF EMERSON'S ESSAYS

8. "In this distribution of functions, the scholar is the delegated intellect. In the right state, he is, *man thinking*. In the degenerate state, when the victim of society, he tends to become a mere thinker, or still worse, the parrot of other men's thinking" (*The Norton Anthology of American Literature*, 244).

Emerson's characterization of a true scholar is a person who is able to self-reliantly move through life and endless whims with grace and a steady brow, all while transcending the past, the present, and the future simultaneously.

A true scholar must be a "university of knowledges" in which he is open to think and reason with the information he has acquired, yet wary when he begins regurgitating information like a parrot.

A true scholar is one who goes "down into the secrets of his own mind" and thus "descend[s] into the secrets of all minds. He learns that he who has mastered any law in his private thoughts, is master to that extent of all men whose language he speaks, and of all into whose language his own can be translated" (252).

A true scholar is not only a person who is book smart but also wise, prudent, sagacious. His wisdom of life pours through all facets, dimensions, and sluices of his own life.

"The office of the scholar is to cheer, raise, and to guide men by showing them facts amidst appearance" (251).

This idyllic universal scholar has pierced the veil of material appearances and has been gifted glimpses into unknown reservoirs of perspective. In this journey through the veil and back, the universal scholar humbly returns with a cup of overflowing wisdom that contains the distilled drops of what he or she can so delicately remember and eagerly share with us all.

"In proportion to the completeness of the distillation, so will the purity and imperishableness of the product be" (246).

In Emerson's view of one's ideal self-reliance, "all the virtues are comprehended" (252). "The world is his who can see through its pretension. What deafness, what stone-blind custom, what overgrown error you behold is there only by sufferance—by your sufferance. See it to be a lie, and you have already dealt it its mortal blow" (252).

Self-reliance, here, is the ability to look at the world with the least amount of necessary ignorance, and the ability to directly gaze at every semblance of darkness without peering away.

For Emerson, this begins by observing one's thoughts and emotions. One who has trouble looking at his inner turmoil will continue with said turmoil and feel undivided within himself and likewise with those around him. Emerson ceaselessly advocates for complete self-trust in oneself, to stare at and to contemplate one's problems whole-heartedly, and fully committing to resolving any distortions found within oneself when appropriate and ready.

"The reason why the world lacks unity, and lies broken and in heaps, is, because man is disunited with himself. He cannot be a naturalist, until he satisfies all the demands of the spirit. Love is as much its demand, as perception" (242).

Love—not egotistical "love"—but love based in one's trust in their inner guidance and in Nature, will grant the keys of wisdom for the self-reliant individual.

"Man is conscious of a universal soul within or behind his individual life, wherein, as in a firmament, the natures of Justice, Truth, Love, Freedom, arise and shine" (223).

In our world, most of us identify our sense of self—of being a permanent person with a name, a history, and a personality—on such a consistent basis, that many believe that their personality and history is *all* of who they really are, and *all* of who they ever will be.

Ralphie is our voice of reason here who attempts to put forth the concept that behind our individual personality is a universal soul where "Truth" and "Beauty" lie (a concept not foreign to metaphysical history, e.g. Plato's Theory of Forms, the Vedanta school of Hinduism's belief in 'Atman' and 'Brahman').

And for one to unlock glimpses of this ideal, one must be able to observe one's thoughts and emotions as a pure unadulterated observer, disidentifying one's sense of identity with the recurring creations of one's thoughts and its associated narratives to see a clearer, more accurate Panorama of Reality.

"But when a faithful thinker, resolute to detach every object from personal relations, and see it in the light of thought, shall, at the same time, kindle science with the fire of the holiest affections, then will God go forth anew into the creation" (242).

In another section, Emerson points out our naïve tendencies in looking back with our rose-colored glasses at the "foregoing generations" who "beheld God and nature face to face" and our obsessive proclivity in viewing knowledge "through their eyes."

This pointing out directly questions why we place so much faith in past generations for their perceptions and views of God / A Higher Power:

"Why should not we also enjoy an original relation to the universe? Why should not we have a poetry and philosophy of insight and not of tradition, and a religion by revelation to us, and not the history of theirs" (214).

This is Emerson's introduction to his "Nature" essay, which immediately catalyzes one's own introspection. He exposes the insanity of giving up our sovereignty to past generations to define our understanding of wisdom, and instead, invites us to start questioning the known while simultaneously plunging headfirst into the Unknown.

In the sphere of art, Emerson believes that "A work of art is an abstract or epitome of the world. It is the result or expression of nature, in miniature. For although the works of nature are innumerable and all different, the result or the expression of them all is similar and single" (222).

Art, with this philosophy now in play, is the attempt to express a slice of nature through any creative medium. And although there are many works of art with varying subject-matters, to Emerson they are all trying to convey the same singular message.

"The poet, the painter, the sculptor, the musician, the architect seek each to concentrate this radiance of the world on one

point, and each in his several work to satisfy the love of beauty which stimulates him to produce" (222).

With this measure of aesthetics, the most beautiful art to Emerson is that which comes closest to suggesting a "universal grace," a feeling of wholeness, a feeling that everything is interconnected, not divided.

"A single object is only so far beautiful as it suggests this universal grace" (222).

Simply, Emerson's ideal universal artist and scholar is a human being so profoundly inspired by the ideals of Beauty & Wholeness that it drives them to fervently "embody it in new forms" while perpetually revealing "the light upon the mystery of humanity."

"TO DIFFERENT MINDS, THE SAME WORLD IS A HELL, AND A HEAVEN."

+ Ralph Waldo Emerson

9. Any semblance of Reality has a noteworthy side effect to it:

 It makes you desire for everyone else to understand and feel this exact feeling of Freedom as well.

 In certain instances of one's Life,

 It will be extremely seductive to believe that Earth is an eternal hell, and at other times, a temporary heaven.

 Yet, you, you yourself are always responsible for believing either view.

 You yourself are always responsible for making yourself feel as free as possible.

 Thus, the highest action you can ever do for yourself and/or another human being is to help them feel freer than they currently think and/or feel right now.

 And even then, there is a more skillful way to express this:

 The highest action you can do for yourself and/or another human being is to remind them that they are already free.

That there is already a place within them where Freedom rings continuously.

That *their very existing* is Freedom ringing Itself.

"You hear the birds?

You see the sun?

Who is not enlightened?"

+ Unknown Zen Master

THIS SILENCED HUM

"…silence is the eternal flow of language."

+ Ramana Maharshi, *Be As You Are*

10. This Silenced Hum is the Ever-Present White Noise of Existence.

Its sound is like that of an empty jar continuously pouring water into itself.

You can even hear it right now.

Just shut the fuck up and listen.

ON DESPAIR

"Now it seems to me that Love of some kind is the only possible explanation of the extraordinary amount of suffering that there is in the world. I cannot conceive any other explanation. I am convinced that there is no other, and that if the worlds have indeed, as I have said, been built out of Sorrow, it has been by the hands of Love…"

+ Oscar Wilde, *De Profundis*

11. Despair is one of our greatest teachers in this Life.

    Once it fully kicks in, you become much less enchanted with the external world and its continuous promises:

    "Hey, over here! Look at me! Look at me!

    This is it! You just need this thing and you'll finally be happy!

    This is it! You just need this experience and you'll finally be fulfilled forever!

    This is it! You just need this lover and you'll be in orgasmic bliss for life!"

    These are the empty promises that replay in our heads when new situations, people, and things enter our lives.

    Yet, once despair kicks in, these promises begin revealing their true colors—or rather, their lack of color.

One, desperately, begins searching for better ways of being, of living in the world, out of immediate necessity.

This simply means that you, now, begin to look for other ways to direct your Attention.

The old ways of being—of existing as a human—of directing your Attention—clearly aren't doing it for you anymore.

You distressingly want to escape these suffocating feelings we properly label despair, frustration, anguish, and suffering because there doesn't seem to be any way out of this claustrophobic clusterfuck.

But slowly, a way out begins to emerge.

A way out of suffering begins to shine its golden rays over the invisible horizon of one's ephemeral self.

Despair begins illuminating your dark and muddled modus operandi.

It begins showing you the mistaken assumptions you were previously, and still, operating from:

That an internal or external experience would ultimately fulfill you.

That an internal or external object would ultimately fulfill you.

That an internal or external person, or identity, would ultimately fulfill you.

Despair ultimately shows you that nothing external will fulfill you.

And neither will anything internal.

Why?

Because *you* are operating from a *you*.

You think *you* is actually real.

And all that perception usually leads to is a perpetual disappointment with a fictional identity, and its distorted perceptions and stories of the world, that continues subtly grasping onto, and desperately hoping, something will finally fulfill its fragmentariness someday.

But the thing is this:

No activity, person, job, object, sensation, pleasure, thought, emotion, feeling, desire, nor experience—whether internal or external—can ever permanently fulfill you.

    And this is just how the Whole Game is structured.

But please, don't believe me solely based on blind faith and on the basis of these words.

Please, test it out for yourself.

I'll be here.

Patiently waiting.

"Our existence has no foundation on which to rest except the transient present. Thus its form is essentially unceasing *motion*, without any possibility of that repose which we continually strive after. It resembles the course of a man running down a mountain who would fall over if he tried to stop and can stay on his feet only by running on; or a pole balanced on the tip of the finger; or a planet which would fall into its sun if it ever ceased to plunge irresistibly forward. Thus existence is typified by unrest."

+ Arthur Schopenhauer, "On the Vanity of Existence"

"The reason everything looks beautiful is because it is out of balance, but its background is always in perfect harmony. This is how everything exists in the realm of Buddha nature, losing its balance against a background of perfect balance."

+
Shunryu Suzuki, *Zen Mind, Beginner's Mind*

GRASPING BUTTERFLIES OF STARDUST

12. There's this predominant belief by our global collective—whether conscious or not—that what we're all searching for to ultimately fulfill us is:

    Out there.

    One of the primary reasons for this, according to my experience so far, seems to be because we feel fragmented in our bodies—the vehicle that allows us to experience this Perplexity of Life.

    And since we don't know how to consciously allow and fully enjoy our natural state of Existingness, to peacefully radiate by itself in our own body, we have thus projected this ideal sense of Wholeness onto our external world, hoping that we will either find this Ideal Wholeness through time:

    The past and/or future.

    Or,

    Through space:

    People, places, objects, and experiences.

Attempting to find this ideal sense of Wholeness through our transient world made up of evanescent thoughts, objects, feelings, emotions, peoples, and experiences is insanity.

The gateway to fulfillment begins in our body, with our Full Attention.

"The human body in its beauty, as the highest potency of all the beauty of material objects, seemed to him just then to be a matter no longer, but, having taken celestial fire, to assert itself as indeed the true, though visible, soul or spirit in things."

+ Walter Pater, *Marius the Epicurean*

Whether it's through forms of entertainment, careers, relationships, food, drink, sports, hobbies, art, shopping, or any other thing we enjoy doing:

We must understand that they are all mere party tricks for us to more intimately enter, enjoy, and be more aware of our earthly body—our personal sanctuary on this planet.

Everything we do is geared towards this aim of entering, enjoying, and being more aware of our body.

And why is this?

Because our body is the gateless gate to what inspirits us, to what gives us Pure Unsullied Life:

This shapelessly interminable, diaphanous feeling of free space.

Our bodies act as both the midwife and the vehicle for this realization and enjoyment.

Fully enter your *entire* body right now, with your Fullest Awareness possible and see if you could feel your *simple existingness*.

This feeling is nothing to be achieved, but only to be allowed, felt, and enjoyed.

It is not an accomplishment, it is a direct realization of what you are from a moment-to-moment basis:

Spacial Vibrating Existingness.

The continuous resting *in* and *as* one's *entire* body is a continuous practice in trust.

And the more trust *in* and *as* one's *entire* body, the more trust in Others, and in one's world.

See what happens when you become aware of the inside and outside of your body.

Just accepting Life as it is.

Effortless Effort.

Including everything that arises in your experience:

Every tension,

Every feeling,

Every thought,

Every sensation,

Every comfort,

Every discomfort.

Allow it into your body.

Allow it to penetrate your Full Awareness.

Integrate it. Coalesce it.

If one excludes and/or attempts to push any of these away, it automatically creates a greater sense of duality:

> *Twoness Tension:*

An imagined someone pushing an imagined something else away.

And thus, the origin of a believed-to-be-self (an ego):

1. Sentient space (one's natural state as Open Attention) existing in and as the body.

2. A constricting of the body and one's Sentient Space occurs. This Sentient Space, which was previously Open Attention transforms itself into a seemingly split and narrow form of Attention.

3. A narrow form of Attention then catalyzes a proliferation of thoughts convincing one to believe that they are *a someone struggling with a something else.*

4. Once this dynamic plays out for however long—of Open Attention believing in its temporary narrowness, and the convincing stories and identities born through it—one returns back to one's natural state of Open Attention until the constricting of the body and one's Sentient Space returns and this vicious cycle repeats itself in infinitesimal intervals.

(This cycle is repeatedly playing throughout our "normal" days without even the slightest clue that this is occurring. Go ahead and feel your body right now. Which parts are you subtly clenching? Which parts are you subtly ignoring?)

Through this model, one can better understand the double-edged sword that is self-examining oneself through thought and logic.

One's directed Attention on self-analyzing thoughts and emotions reinforces the creation and self-analyzing of more thoughts and emotions ad infinitum.

An activity that is meant to get closer to Truth, to Wholeness, to Simple Vibrating Existingness, ironically pushes one further away.

It automatically creates a split, a separation:

Me & Truth.

Seeker & Sought.

Knower & Known.

Observer & Observed.

Subject & Object.

The very seeking creates the duality, the separation.

The seeking creates a sense of two-ness and reinforces an "illusory me" struggling to overcome an "illusory something else."

"Awareness of all of this, which is real meditation, has revealed that there is a central image put together by all the other images, and this central image, the observer, is the censor, the experiencer, the evaluator, the judge who wants to conquer or subjugate the other images or destroy them altogether. The other images are the result of judgments, opinions and conclusions by the observer, and the observer is the result of all the other images—therefore the observer is the observed."

+ Jiddu Krishnamurti, *Freedom from the Known*

The point to belabor here is this:

It is only one's Free & Open Attention in disguise pretending to be both parties every single time.

In reality, there are no problems that actually exist.

Problems are only problems because we believe them to be problems.

MOVING WITH CIRCULAR MOMENTUM

13. When an experience arises within our Attention:

    Whether a thought, a feeling, a desire, or a sensation,

    We tend to move with them without our conscious approval.

    This is true of what has constituted most of our human experience so far:

    Believing that our thoughts, feelings, and sensations are real, permanent, and substantial.

    So, what is it that always moves in tandem with an experience?

    Our Attention.

    Thus the importance of being attentive when a thought, a feeling, a desire, and/or sensation begins to move through you.

    Acknowledge its presence. Notice its movements and character.

    See if you actually do want to move with that specific thought, feeling, desire, and/or sensation.

    What story is it trying to convince you in believing this time?

    Which identity is it trying to convince you that you are this time?

With our active noticing, other ways of reacting to and understanding our experiences naturally reveal themselves.

This is the official introduction to recognizing a new kind of freedom we didn't know we possessed.

"Meditation doesn't entail the suppression of such thoughts, but it does require that we notice thoughts as they emerge and recognize them to be transitory appearances in consciousness. In subjective terms, you are consciousness itself—you are not the next, evanescent image or string of words that appears in your mind. Not seeing it arise, however, the next thought will seem to become what you are."

+ Sam Harris, *Waking Up*

FILIBUSTERING IDENTITY

14.   A sense of identity cries for its need of necessity.

And readily the entity wallows in its enmity selfishly.

Paradoxically forgetting the duality of one's density,

Seemingly changes the polarity momentarily,

While intuitively remembering a fluxing transparency,

Subjectively stills the identity propensity.

UNDER THE GUISE OF SOCIAL

15. Our world for thousands of years now,

    Including this contemporaneous era,

    Is the stunning epitome of the blind leading the blind.

    And to go even further, and a bit harsher:

    The blind enslaving the blind.

    We currently live in an attention economy that persistently attempts—by various competing characters—to hijack and influence our Attention.

    Twitter, Facebook, Instagram, and all forms of social media are our contemporary hijackers who can be considered to be *the digital clones of our minds* recreated out in the world.

    From this line of thinking, each social media application can be considered to be one giant mind filled with millions and billions of thoughts.

    Each person's profile represents the various regions of the one giant mind.

    And each post, comment, and/or activity from a person's profile represents the thoughts and activity of the one giant mind.

Within this dynamic, we are being both exploited and given exactly what we want.

Just as we function in our day-to-day, moment-to-moment lives:

Reacting to activity in different regions of our brain, and to our thoughts and their respective associations,

We are doing the same exact thing on social media:

Reacting to various people's profiles (activity in different regions of our brain), and to their posts, comments, and other activity (thoughts and associations).

From a detached point of view, it's truly mesmerizing.

And from an attached point of view, it's utterly horrendous.

Many predominantly flock to social media because it gives them the illusion that they are able to choose their own friends and what they see on a daily basis, which carries the implicit assumption that you are simultaneously able to change your habitual thoughts and its patterns.

Social media provides the perfectly nuanced distraction from confronting one's thoughts and the associated mental patterns one has yet to observe and properly understand.

The whole thing seems so natural though, mostly due to social media's biomimicry of our thinking processes.

But in reality, its a drug in which we're sadly unaware of our own addiction.

Or even worse:

An addiction we don't want to readily admit to.

In its final analysis, the natural thinking system needs to be reconciled from its root system.

Not from its simulacrum.

"So you should observe that which naturally arises and naturally originates within your own [mind]. [First], observe [the source] from which these appearances initially originated, [Second, observe the place] in which they abide in the interim, And [third, observe the place] to which they will finally go."

+ *The Tibetan Book of the Dead*

SWIRLING VOICES OF THE RESPLENDENT WHIRLPOOL

16. We all enjoy consuming different forms of media such as: movies, music, books, magazines, TV shows, the internet, podcasts, videos, articles, seminars, social media, and other mediums of communication because *we are looking for permission.*

    We are all yearning to find that person and/or concept who has expressed similar thoughts, attitudes, and/or ideas we have either had before and never expressed ourselves,

    Or conversely, thoughts, attitudes, and/or ideas we have never had before and want to now act upon.

    We want someone to express these kind of thoughts, attitudes, and/or ideas so that we can finally allow ourselves the freedom to openly express them with our own world.

    Essentially:

    We are looking for our own idealized templates that we believe will finally allow us to live a freer, creative, and more authentic way of Life.

"But idealization which is art has the benefit of holding a clarifying mirror up to Nature. It shows us by deliberate artifice what is potentially in Nature to be seen, in life to be felt, in speculation to be thought."

+ Irwin Edman, *Arts and the Man*

A KNOWING WILLINGNESS

17. Confidence in one's intuitions.

A gallant *willingness* to risk and apply them in yourself and in your world.

An ardent *willingness* of not being afraid "to fail."

A shrewd *knowingness* that there is no such thing as failure.

An intimate *knowingness* that *you will never have all the answers.*

And in that *Knowing Willingness* you will have found freedom from freedom.

"Always trust yourself and your own feeling, as opposed to argumentation, discussions, or introductions of that sort; if it turns out that you are wrong, then the natural growth of your inner life will eventually guide you to other insights. Allow your judgements their own silent, undisturbed development, which, like all progress, must come from deep within and cannot be forced or hastened. Everything is gestation and then birthing. To let each impression and each embryo of a feeling come to completion, entirely in itself, in the dark, in the unsayable, the unconscious, beyond the reach of one's own understanding, and with deep humility and patience to wait for the hour when a new clarity is born: this alone is what it means to live as an artist: in understanding as in creating."

+ Rainer Maria Rilke, *Letters to a Young Poet*

BORROW EVERYTHING

18. Borrow every meaningful idea you can possibly find.

And make it entirely your own.

"Truth and reason are common to all men, and no more belong to the man who first uttered them than to him that repeated them after him. It is no more a matter of Plato's opinion than of mine, when he and I understand and see things alike. The bees steal from this flower and that, but afterwards turn their pilferings into honey, which is their own; it is thyme and marjoram no longer. So the pupil will transform and fuse together the passages that he borrows from others, to make of them something entirely his own; that is to say, his own judgement."

> \+ Michel de Montaigne, *Essays*,
> "On the Education of Children"

"The base of all artistic genius is the power of conceiving humanity in a new, striking, rejoicing way, of putting a happy world of its own creation in place of the meaner world of common days, of generating around itself an atmosphere with a novel power of refraction, selecting, transforming, recombining the images it transmits, according to the choice of the imaginative intellect."

+ Walter Pater, *Studies in the History of the Renaissance*

A PARTIALLY INCOMPLETE OUTLINE OF TOLSTOY'S *WHAT IS ART?*

(Excerpt from *Criticism: Major Statements*)

19.

Title: *What is Art?*

Author: Leo Tolstoy

Abstract:

What is art? What is the purpose of art? These are two primary questions that Tolstoy poses for readers and himself in an extract of his book: *What Is Art?* found in *Criticism: Major Statements* (4th edition).

"Art, all art, has this characteristic, that it unites people" (387).

This is Tolstoy's predominant message throughout the entirety of his tract: *unity*. Simply, there is 'good' art that unites and there is 'bad' art that divides. Tolstoy is entirely repulsed by bad art and leaves no room for it anywhere in society:

"…bad art, deserving not to be encouraged but to be driven out, denied, and despised, as being art not uniting but dividing people" (392).

Outline:

I. This excerpt of *What Is Art?* begins with the question, "How in the subject-matter of art are we to decide what is good and what is bad?" The question that has haunted generations of poets, philosophers, and artists is now being tackled by Tolstoy. This is his first attempt in answering it: "Art like speech is a means of communication and therefore of progress, that is, of the movement of humanity forward towards perfection" (383).

- a. He proceeds to put speech, as a means of communication, into a universal perspective: "Speech renders accessible to men of the latest generations all the knowledge discovered by the experience and reflection both of preceding generations and of the best and foremost men of their own times" (383). He continues, "…art renders accessible to men of the latest generations all the feelings experienced by their predecessors and also those felt by their best and foremost contemporaries" (383).

- b. With this foundation, Tolstoy proceeds to elucidate his views on art's purpose as: "…the evolution of knowledge proceed[ing] by truer and more necessary knowledge dislodging and replacing what was mistaken and unnecessary, so the evolution of feeling proceeds by means of art—feelings less kind and less necessary for the well-being of mankind being replaced by others kinder and more needful for that end. That is the purpose of art" (383).

II. With Tolstoy now including feeling and emotion into the equation, he also begins to integrate his favored theme of brotherhood in relation to art's purpose: "…the consciousness that our well-being, both material and spiritual, individual and collective, temporal and eternal, lies in the growth of brotherhood among men—in their loving harmony with one another" (385). This is where he begins to make repeated references to God, Christianity, and brotherhood.

a. "Christian art is such only as tends to unite all without exception..." (387). Although it begins to seem as if Tolstoy is pushing a Christian agenda here, he goes on to further explain what art shouldn't be, or do, in relation to faith: "It must be the art not of some one group of people, or of one class, or of one nationality, or of one religious cult; that is, it must not transmit feelings accessible only to a man educated in a certain way, or only to an aristocrat, or a merchant, or only to a Russian, or a native of Japan, or a Roman Catholic, or a Buddhist, and so on, but it must transmit feelings accessible to everyone" (387).

III. For Tolstoy "only two kinds of feeling do unite all men: first, feelings flowing from perception of our sonship to God and of the brotherhood of man; and next, the simple feelings of common life accessible to every one without exception—such as feelings of merriment, of pity, of cheerfulness, of tranquility, and so forth" (388). These are the requirements for 'good' art in his opinion.

    a. Along with the feelings of the "perception of our sonship to God and brotherhood of man," Tolstoy also calls for: "...a feeling of sureness in truth, devotion to the will of God, self-sacrifice, respect for and love of man..." (388).

IV. To emphasize once again, in terms of 'bad' art, Tolstoy believes it is "...not to be encouraged but to be driven out, denied, and despised, as being art not uniting but dividing people" (392). Through his work one can see Tolstoy's insistence on bad art being completely void and null. In his view, bad art is the epitome of all the confusion and sin found in both the individual and collective world.

Response:

In all, Tolstoy's inquiry: What is art? has led him to disclose opinions that art should solely be used to progress humanity and unite the brotherhood of man through speech, feeling, understanding, and emotion. He also relays his important message in which the ideal of religious art should transmit "…both positive feelings of love of God and one's neighbor, and negative feelings of indignation and horror at the violation of love" (389). Art should ultimately *include, not exclude*. And finally, if it wasn't already enough, Tolstoy gifts us a worthwhile reflection when contemplating the worth of any piece of art:

"Whatever the work may be and however it may have been extolled, we have first to ask whether this work is one of real art, or a counterfeit" (393).

ELIMINATING TIME'S MONOPOLY

> "I hear time fall,
> drop by drop,
> and not one drop that falls can be heard."
>
> + Fernando Pessoa, *The Book of Disquiet*

20. *We are all fervently searching for our way out of time.*

For the entirety of our Lives, we continuously perform actions that we believe will best eliminate our perception of time.

We yearn for and search for those timeless activities that allow us to expose time's monopoly on our Attention.

We prefer and value these activities over all others because we know how paltry and limiting living in time feels.

Or more accurately said:

We prefer and value these timeless activities over all others because we know how paltry and limiting living *in the perception of time* feels.

We already know Timelessness exists.

And how do we know this?

Because we live every second of it within this industrial manmade framework of a 24-hour schema.

Because we've all experienced that feeling of freedom in which we felt we escaped the clutches of the *concept* of time.

Timelessness is our very Nature.

Freedom is our very Nature.

Yet, our problem is this:

We *think* we have to "get back" to Timelessness somehow.

We *think* we have to "get back" to Freedom somehow.

We delude ourselves into believing that we have lost our own Inherent Freedom, our own Innate Nature, and now, we need to go on a long, meaningful, and strenuous search for it.

And, therein lies the whole problem:

A *someone* trying to get back *somewhere*.

A *someone* trying to get back *something*.

When we should really be asking ourselves the questions:

Who's trying to get back *where*?

Who's trying to get back *what*?

"We are not to become something—we are already it. This is the whole message of all the awakened ones—that you are not to achieve something; it has already been given to you. It is a gift from existence. You are already where you should be; you can't be anywhere else. There is nowhere to go, nothing to achieve. [And] Because there is nowhere to go and nothing to achieve, you can celebrate. Then there is no hurry, no worry, no anxiety, no anguish, no fear of being a failure. You can't fail. In the very nature of things, it is impossible to fail, because there is no question of success at all."

+ Osho, *Fame, Fortune, & Ambition*

FINDING NEW PATTERNS IN THE PALATIAL PATTERN

"Until the late modern era, more than 90 percent of humans were peasants who rose each morning to till the land by the sweat of their brows. The extra they produced fed the tiny minority of elites—kings, government officials, soldiers, priests, artists and thinkers—who fill the history books. History is something that very few people have been doing while everyone else was ploughing fields and carrying water buckets."

+ Yuval Noah Harari, *Sapiens*

21. People in our current society are usually rewarded to the degree they help others *forget, escape, and/or save time,* whether it's through:

    - Entertainment: actors, athletes, singers, musicians, dancers, directors, producers, performers, writers, etcetera etcetera.

    - Art: music, movies, books, paintings, sculptures, television, videos, podcasts, social media, etcetera etcetera.

    - Entrepreneurial and/or scientific endeavors: Inventing a product, a game, a medicine, a company, a service. Investing in businesses, markets, and ideas.

    - And lastly, working for a company or government.

Fortune tends to favor and reward those who rebel from the customary and unlock new combinations in the Universe.

DON'T PANIC

22. As one begins Life, one begins reaching out for warmth, security, and what's needed to survive.

    As one progresses in age, these reaching-outs tend to increase in extravagance and superfluity while simultaneously attempting to avoid anything unpleasant.

    As one matures—and if intelligent enough—one will develop reaching-outs for *only* what is needed and *accepting the unpleasant and unexpected* in any packaging it comes wrapped in, that is, with balanced equanimity and an unshakable understanding.

    The underlying premise for these reaching-outs seems to be an unnerving feeling of lack and limit we feel within ourselves.

    We seemingly forget that we, Consciousness, are timeless and infinite in essence.

    But the trouble we get ourselves into, by even admitting that we, Consciousness, are timeless and infinite, is the simultaneous tacit admission that time and finiteness actually exist, that there is something *other* than Consciousness.

    Thus, I write all of this, out of my Unconditional Love for myself and for future generations,

    So that I can tell you, sincerely and directly:

    That neither time nor finity exists, and neither does timelessness nor infinity as well.

Time transcends Time.

Finity transcends Finity.

Timelessness transcends Timelessness.

And Infinity transcends Infinity.

"The vanity of existence is revealed in the whole form existence assumes: in the infiniteness of time and space contrasted with the finiteness of the individual in both; in the fleeting present as the sole form in which actuality exists; in the contingency and relativity of all things; in continual becoming without being; in continual desire without satisfaction; in the continual frustration of striving of which life consists."

+ Arthur Schopenhauer, *Essays and Aphorisms*

The Whole Macrocosm is the Whole Microcosm.

The Whole Microcosm is the Whole Macrocosm.

Perpetually creating a Universal Synecdoche that is our inviolable matrix code:

The Whole embodying the Fragment and the Fragment embodying the Whole.

ANOTHER DAY ALIVE

"The days melt in my hands like ice in the sun."

+ Honoré de Balzac

23. Another day in space.

    Another day in time.

    Another day in no-space.

    Another day in no-time.

    Another day in body.

    Another day in soul.

    Another day in This

    Another day in That.

Another day on Earth.

Another day in Space.

Another day in Form.

Another day in No Form.

Another day in this Moment.

Another day in the Next Moment.

Another day alive.

Another day alive.

SPURIOUS ENVISAGINGS

24. "Looky here," the old geyser winded, "today is no different than yesterday.

    Only *today's today* is enough for 2,000 elephants to pass through comfortably."

    Do we have it yet? Tomorrow's lunch for the rest of the year?

    Not quite.

    More is needed if I ever hope to tune this tuba to the desired frequency of the Universal Tape Measure.

    Nebulas of thought race across the Milky Way of my nebulous mind-space, frolicking with the airs of a Persian flute player who prefers grapes over ostentatiousness.

    Sound the soundboard with a painter's toothbrush!

    Milk the airwaves for everything they've got!

    Follow the meaning of these words with nonchalant dexterity!

    See that no word is unturned in its cornucopia of advances and proposals!

    See that everyone gets a promotion for doing absolutely nothing!

A MEMORANDUM FOR SOME COLLEGE STUDENTS

"I wonder if we have ever asked ourselves what education means. Why do we go to school, why do we learn various subjects, why do we pass examinations and compete with each other for better grades? What does this so-called education mean, and what is it all about?…Why do we go through the struggle to be educated?"

+ Jiddu Krishnamurti, *Think on These Things*

25. "I" wakes up.

   Who's "I?"

   Or, rather, "What is 'I'?"

   "I" is a word, a concept, an idea.

   It's present within time,

   It's present within space,

   It's present within a body,

   Within a room,

Within a house,

Within a family,

Within a state,

Within a country,

Within a continent,

Within a planet,

Within a solar system,

Within a galaxy,

Within a Universe,

And finally, within this Cosmic I Don't Know.

"I" is currently using time in this Life to experience the college journey as a student.

This college journey is an experience in which students, teachers, and faculty members (other "I"s) connect and transfer knowledge, wisdom, and energy with one another.

All of us "I's" mutually agree on this concept of college, and thus, its students pay the business—the college—thousands of dollars of paper and electronic currency in hopes to someday be rewarded with a rectangular piece of paper with inscribed letters of our English alphabet, indicating that this "I" has completed the business' requirements for certification and is now ready to join the workforce of many other "I's" with similar rectangular pieces of paper containing related words and meanings.

Now, "I" does not intend to undermine our current educational institutions, or in any way promote a morose view of the above didactic deconstruction of college (in this essay, at least), but "I" does propose the opposite effect:

Attempting to convey the significance of a deeper and more profound understanding that is often overlooked, which is the notion that:

We are all experiencing this journey of Life together.

And more specifically:

This journey of college together.

At least four days out of the week, we gather together into the same building with joint intentions of learning about our world and history herself.

We hope to learn something from Life's most interesting characters who have breathed, walked, and shit on this planet before.

From its most respected writers, historians, scientists, poets, philosophers, and their remarkable and/or inane ideas.

We go to class, listen to the lecture, take notes, and then work on an assignment.

Then what?

Are we actually happy through all of this?

What's the point? What's the end goal, if there is one?

Well, the ancient Greeks and many other wisdom lovers, namely Aristotle, believed and attempted to cultivate something called:

Eudaimonia.

A concept we'll simply define here as: *the state of one's flourishing, happiness, and well-being as an individual.*

Essentially, Aristotle believed that there was a formula for reaching one's highest human good (supposedly).

In his eyes, it is through the embodiment of certain virtues such as: courage, temperance, liberality, magnificence, magnanimity, proper ambition, patience, wittiness, friendliness, modesty, righteous indignation, and truthfulness that would bring one closer to a quintessential happiness and health.

Now, quoting and pretending to clearly understand Aristotle is cute and all, but more importantly, how can one tap into their own potential *eudaimonia* during college?

Frankly, "I" can't pretend to know—and advice is usually pretty cheap when unasked for—but what "I" can do is deconstruct some deeply-ingrained thoughts on our current educational expectations, processes, and our personal relation to them.

So first:

Why are you in college?

Societal convention?

Pressure from your parents, friends, relatives?

Out of your own volition?

Second: Why are you in the major you're in?

Societal convention?

Pressure from your parents, friends, relatives?

Out of your own volition?

Third: Do you get excited to go to school or do you curse every single second you're there?

Fourth: Why do you get excited? Or, why do you curse every single second you're there?

Go deeply into these questions, don't let them pass by uncontemplated.

Why is there this common festering of discontent and dejection within our current perception of school?

One grudgingly waiting for that glorious graduation day and glorified rectangle that will somehow magically fix all of one's anxieties and apprehensions of the future?

To fully milk the precious time one has during their college journey, it's important to pause and reflect on the more profound reflections of Life from time to time:

"Out of all of the places I could be, why am I here?"

"Out of all the things I could be doing, why this?"

"Out of all the possible combinations in our society, and similarly within this Galaxy, why is *this* status quo currently the status quo? Why am I choosing to blindly follow it? Why am I choosing to go against it?"

Contemporary philosopher and author Alain de Botton offers us some possible consolation:

"But it is not only the hostility of others that may prevent us from questioning the status quo. Our will to doubt can be just as powerfully sapped by an internal sense that societal conventions must have a sound basis, even if we are not sure exactly what this may be, because they have been adhered to by a great many people for a long time. It seems implausible that our society could be gravely mistaken in its beliefs and at the same time that we would be alone in noticing the fact."

As a senior, "I's" college journey has included a three-year business stint, in which he loathed almost every minute of it.

Not necessarily because of the teachers, nor the program, but because it wasn't resonant with this "I."

The right questions weren't asked and investigated beforehand.

It wasn't until his senior year that "I" intensely contemplated his present situation and switched to the English program, learning more substance in one year than those previous three years bound together.

And why is that?

Well, for a surplus of better ways of phrasing this:

"I" actually gave a shit about what he was learning.

The "standard" view of one's college journey seems to be that one only needs to attend classes and properly complete assignments to pass and finally graduate to what seems like a glorious liberation from a soul-destroying prison.

But the frequently overlooked aspect is this:

We are already liberated!

We are given an opportunity to spend around four years thinking, observing, and maturing in an environment of like-minded and, a couple, superior-minded peers.

Yet most squander this precious gift, feeling victimized and grumbling at how miserable their current state of affairs is.

What cruel irony, one is paying thousands of dollars to be miserable?

16th- century French philosopher and writer, Michel de Montaigne, offers us a poignant question when contemplating if one's education has sincerely served its purpose:

> "'Has he [the student] become better and wiser?' We ought to find out not who understands most but who understands best. We work merely to fill the memory, leaving the understanding and the sense of right and wrong empty."

So how does the student become better and wiser? How will they understand best?

This whole college journey is a course in wisdom and knowledge in its every dimension:

An interaction with a stranger in the concourse,

A lecture on the gender politics of Malaysian mollusks,

An intimate hug by a friend,

Devouring that spongy, red velvet cupcake from the cafe,

That party two Saturdays ago,

That assignment on psychoanalyzing Edgar Allen Poe's *The Cask of Amontillado*,

Overhearing a passive aggressive discussion between two colleagues in the library.

And even, watching your friend incessantly fidget after consuming four cups of coffee in less than two hours.

These seemingly mundane everyday experiences are the very roots of our education and wisdom.

We take them to be the most insignificant events, when really, they are the grandest.

These occurrences graciously lend themselves as mirrors to reflect one's current state of "I," and the opportunity to recognize the grandeur of each passing moment's creative happenings.

What if our classes and assignments were just mediums for us to better understand the perceptions of ourself and of our world? To help us become better human beings?

What if *eudaimonia* is not something to be gained, but something already present, only waiting to be recognized, shared, and freely enjoyed with others?

We must change our contemporary perception, both in the individual and in the collective lens, of how we view schooling as a societal and servile duty to memorize facts and somnambulantly drudge through.

We must adopt a more comprehensive perception of the college journey as a vehicle for our own awakening, of becoming better human beings.

This isn't to dismiss one's previous and future suffering as whimsical and unnecessary, but instead, to transmute one's suffering, and understand its horrifyingly beautiful dynamics.

As "I" now departs from college to the next stage of his unfolding, he hopes to leave some insights which have aided his own "I" and might possibly aid another's:

- Observe what classes you actually enjoy attending and recognize why.

- Pick classes, and ultimately a major, that you naturally gravitate towards, despite their connotations and stereotypes.

- Find your strengths, what you're intuitively good at.

- Acknowledge your weaknesses.

- Hang out with every kind of people.

- Try out various clubs, events, and activities.
- Get to know your professors (they're humans too).
- Travel.
- Write.
- Dance.
- Paint.
- Observe.
- Breathe!
- Question.
- Drink quality water.
- Research the greatest wisdom, ideas, and people that have graced this very Earth.
- Say yes more than no.
- Consciously challenge your preconceived limits.

- Continuously observe and make nice with one's thoughts and its bewildering processes.

- Understand the true nature of suffering.

- Become cozy with the fact of your inevitable death.

- Trust the spontaneous unfolding.

- And Love.

- Love.

- Love.

Follow Love to wherever Love leads you.

INTERMISSION

FEAR IS ONLY A CERTAIN KIND OF ENERGY

> "The world is constantly confronting us with the truth.
> We are constantly withdrawing....
> We choose to trade off reality for the safety of our cage."
>
> + Stephen Levine, *Who Dies?*

26. When fear arises within your experience, within your Attention, does it not make its presence known as *a certain kind of feeling*?

    And when a *feeling* arises within your experience, within your Attention, is it not only *a certain kind of energy* that we have learned to label with a word?

    For example:

    Happiness is experienced as a certain kind of energy, with its distinct vibrational signature, that arises and then passes after some moments.

    Anger is experienced as a certain kind of energy, with its distinct vibrational signature, that arises and then passes after some moments.

    In the same way, isn't fear also experienced as a certain kind of energy, with its distinct vibrational signature, that arises within our experience and then passes after some moments?

Fear, in its purest essence, is only a certain kind of energy that makes its forceful presence known within our experience, within our body, within our Attention, for a few insignificant moments and eventually passes like everything else in this Life.

"The soul that is elevated and well regulated, that passes through any experience as if it counted for comparatively little, that smiles at all the things we fear or pray for, is impelled by a force that comes from heaven."

> + Seneca, *Letters From a Stoic*, Letter XLI

THE UNDERLYING PREMISE OF REALITY

"Whatever the needs of the moment, I had a choice: I could do what was required calmly, patiently, and attentively, or do it in a state of panic. Every moment of the day—indeed, every moment throughout one's life—offers an opportunity to be relaxed and responsive or to suffer unnecessarily."

+ Sam Harris, *Waking Up*

27. The underlying premise in any moment, practice, study, and/or activity we undertake is to find out which aspects of Reality we openly accept,

    Which aspects we vigorously deny,

    And why.

"The poet makes himself a *visionary* through a long, a prodigious and rational disordering of *all* the senses. Every form of love, of suffering, of madness; he searches himself, he consumes all the poisons in him, keeping only their quintessences."

+ Arthur Rimbaud, *Illuminations*

THE MIND'S UTILITARIAN PURPOSE & ITS FINAL FRONTIER

28. Our rational minds are useful for mainly 3 things:

    1. For one's survival.

    2. For one's normal day-to-day functioning.

    &

    3. To realize and accept its wonderfully fortunate limitation to ever go beyond itself.

* * *

Remind yourself of this whenever needed:

Life is always much, much more than we merely conceptualize so.

HAVE YOU EVER WATCHED A BABY BREATHE?

"The True Man breathes with his heels;
the mass of men breathe with their throats."

+ Chuang-Tzu

29. It seems as if when our Attention does not include our *whole* body,

    It naturally concentrates itself in our head where the dormitories of the majority of our senses are located.

    While this is happening, the rest of our body feels numb, dead, and most times, even forgotten.

    As a result, it reinforces the pandemonium of our thought processes, and the associated tightness in the upper part of our body where the preponderance of the energy of our Attention is currently residing.

    If our energy (Attention) doesn't flow as efficiently as it should through our *entire* vehicle (our body) in this Lifetime, then what can we realistically expect from *the quality of our passing moments*.

"There would seem to be nothing more obvious, more tangible and palpable than the present moment. And yet it eludes us completely. All the sadness of life lies in that fact. In the course of a single second, our senses of sight, of hearing, of smell, register (knowingly or not) a swarm of events and a parade of sensations and ideas passes through our head. Each instant represents a little universe irrevocably forgotten in the next instant."

+ Milan Kundera, *The Art of the Novel*

WE ARE SPACE & ONLY SPACE

"You are just pure space in which millions of processes exist, in which life flows with all its processes and you remain uncorrupted by it….Once you understand yourself as pure space and many things happening, you become detached. Then you become fearless, because there is nothing to lose, there is nobody to lose anything."

+ Osho, *The Art of Living and Dying*

30. The only way to *know* space is to *be* space,

And the only way to *be* space is to *feel* space.

"IS IT REALLY GOD THAT CREATED MAN, OR IS THE OPPOSITE?"

+ Khalil Gibran

31. Did we ultimately create the concept of God as a way to stop us from killing ourselves?

    Or is there an innate part of ourselves that always remembers a *Higher something* of which we come from and continuously attempt to seek for and express in our world?

    It seems as if we have placed all of our faith, belief, and hope-ish energy into our egos, meaning: a believed-to-be-self:

    A continuity of thoughts and sensations perpetually convincing itself that it is *actually someone* solid and non-fluxing,

    Which, in its similar mechanics, has, in turn, created a *believe-to-be-god* who rules over us and the rest of the confusions that follows this line of thinking.

    And thus, because the bulk of us think our individuality is *actually someone concrete, everlasting, and permanent,* then there *must obviously* be some godly personality(s) who must be very similar—but a little better and more virtuous of course.

"When you say you love God what does it mean?
It means that you love a projection of your own imagination, a projection of yourself clothed in certain forms of respectability according to what you think is noble and holy…"

+ Jiddu Krishnamurti, *Freedom From the Known*

However, equally parallel to this:

It would seem like the pinnacle of folly to claim that *something* hasn't created all of *this:*

Look, even Voltaire agrees with me:

"It is natural to admit the existence of a God as soon as one opens one's eyes…The creation betokens the Creator. It is by virtue of an admirable art that all the planets dance round the sun. Animals, vegetables, minerals—everything is ordered with proportion, number, movement. Nobody can doubt that a painted landscape or drawn animals are works of skilled artists. Could copies possibly spring from an intelligence and the originals not?"

"That nostalgia for unity, that appetite for the absolute illustrates the essential impulse of the human drama."

+ Albert Camus, *The Myth of Sisyphus*

I AM, THEREFORE I AM

32.

I think, therefore I am.

It's an admirable attempt, but Descartes had to know that it was going to evolve at some point.

What immediately comes to mind is to flip it:

I am, therefore I think.

But as I ponder it deeper, it becomes:

I am, therefore I am.

"Cartesian thought began with an attempt to reach God as object by starting from the thinking self. But when God becomes object, he sooner or later 'dies,' because God as object is unthinkable. God as object is not only a mere abstract concept, but one which contains so many internal contradictions that it becomes entirely nonnegotiable except when it is hardened into an idol that is maintained in existence by a sheer act of will. For a long time man continued to be capable of this willfulness: but now the effort has become exhausting and many Christians have realized it to be futile."

+ Thomas Merton, *Zen and the Birds of Appetite*

FLIMSY CARTOGRAPHY

33. Believing in any religion, philosophy, guru, and/or system of thought to come closer to The Truth is akin to standing on top of a treasure chest and asking a cartographer to draw a map of where they think the treasure might be.

"Suppose a warrior, forgetting that he was already wearing his pearl on his forehead, were to seek for it elsewhere, he could travel the whole world without finding it. But if someone who knew what was wrong were to simply point it out to him, the warrior would immediately realize that the pearl had been there all the time.

So, if you students of the Way are mistaken about your own real Mind, not recognizing that it is the Buddha, you will consequently look for him elsewhere, indulging in various achievements and practices and expecting to attain realization by such graduated practices. But, even after aeons of diligent searching, you will not be able to attain to the Way."

\+ Huang-Po,
"The Chün Chou Record of the Zen Master Huang Po"

PHILOSOPHY IS BOTH CRUCIAL & USELESS

34. One studies philosophy for its flaws,

    The marvels of what one has yet to think of and discover,

    And, lastly, for its seductive poetry.

"Philosophy is to be studied, not for the sake of any definite answers to its questions, since no definite answers can, as a rule, be known to be true, but rather for the sake of the questions themselves; because these questions enlarge our conception of what is possible, enrich our intellectual imagination and diminish the dogmatic assurance which closes the mind against speculation…"

+ Bertrand Russell, *The Problems of Philosophy*

"But only philosophy will wake us; only philosophy will shake us out of that heavy sleep. Devote yourself entirely to her. You're worthy of her, she's worthy of you—fall into each other's arms."

+ Seneca, *Letters From a Stoic*, Letter LIII

PHILOSOPHIZING

35. It usually comes to pass that almost every alluring theory or captivating philosophy that you come up with always seems utterly foolproof and inviolable at first…that is…

    Until you have to explain it to others, or even yourself for that matter.

    Yet, one will, nonetheless, continue writing down and contemplating philosophical musings because:

    a) They spontaneously appear within you.

    b) There's an organic proclivity towards these interests.

    c) You believe they are necessary reminders that will help you and others deal with future moments better and with a lesser degree of suffering.

    d) They reveal new questions that usurp one's erroneous beliefs that currently hinder the enjoyment of one's Reality.

    e) There is nothing else that is presently more worthwhile to do.

"Our disputes are about words. I ask what is Nature, Pleasure, a Circle, and Substitution. The question is couched in words, and is answered in the same coin. A stone is a body. But if you press the point: And what is a body? — A substance. — And what is a substance? and so on, you will end by driving the answerer to exhaust his dictionary. One substitutes one word for another that is often less well understood."

+ Michel de Montaigne, *Essays*, "On Experience"

ACTIONLESS DOINGS

36. Seeds.

   Being spread.

   All over.

   For everyone.

   To enjoy.

   To flourish.

   To thrive.

   The seed is deployed.

And that's that.

It's out of your hands.

You have fulfilled your Sacred Duty.

No pride.

No feelings of doership.

No traces.

Nothing.

RECONCILIATIONS OF USING A DREAMED-UP ALPHABET

37. I write because there is something that begs to be reconciled and expressed for some unknown reasoning in this Fragile Instant.

    The same applies to all of my speech, and all of the Art "I" create.

    A recurring reconciling of contradictions.

    That is what Life seems to be at every moment.

    So if any of my writing ever feels as if it lacks any sort of closure, any form of finality, any sort of completeness to it,

    It is most likely that the matter has already begun to resolve within me, and words are no longer needed.

"As for the natural faculties within me, of which my writing is the proof, I feel them bending under the burden. My ideas and my judgement merely grope their way forward, faltering, tripping, and stumbling; and when I have advanced as far as I can, I am still not at all satisfied. I can see more country ahead, but with so disturbed and clouded a vision that I can distinguish nothing."

> + Michel de Montaigne, *Essays*,
> "On the Education of Children"

ON FORCING INSPIRATION

38. During this vacillating voyage through space-time we call Reality, there will be phases wherein:

    Creativity will gush through your very fingertips deprived of any iota of effort and/or mental strain.

    Inspiration will seem to flush through your being like a golden fountain of cascading effervescence,

    And synchronicity will align your fate with the stars, connecting you with the right people(s), ideas, things, and situations that seemed unimaginable and/or out of reach before.

    While, *at other times*, the diametrical opposite of all these things will be painfully obvious and apparent, including:

    Perpetually placing 1st in every Mental Gynamstics & Cognitive Acrobatics World Championship,

    Wanting to rip out every cell and sub-atomic molecule from the flesh that was loaned to you,

    And ceaselessly doubting if any ounce of creativity and/or inspiration will ever grace your being ever again.

    So, regardless of wherever you might be, and whatever it might be, *keep on doing as you feel best.*

    Console yourself with the notion that everything, including Nature and the arranged dynamics of our Universe, works in cycles.

"My advice therefore is that one should not force anything; it is better to fritter away one's unproductive days and hours, or sleep through them, than to try at such time to write something which will give one no satisfaction later on."

+ Johann Wolfgang von Goethe

HOOPLAH

39. If everything is bound to dissolve at some point in this Life,

    including ourselves,

    then what actually matters?

WHAT AN IMMEDIATE SHIFT OF PERCEPTION ONCE DEATH IS CONSIDERED

40. DO YOU NOT UNDERSTAND?!?

This Life Is Too Precious To Waste On Minutiae!

Wake up from your slumber!

Reflect on the fact that we have absolutely no idea how we got here, nor have any idea where we're going after we die!

Savor this Smoothie of Life which keeps on mixing and mixing for our aimless enjoyment and valiant exploration.

Appreciate it's Measureless Immensity with your mind, body, spirit, and everything else you were loaned!

Our misleading perceptions of depression, misery, and the nausea of life seem to be the sustained fooling of ourselves as if we'll be here forever.

Our friends,

Our family,

Our beliefs,

Our behaviors,

Our ambitions,

Our routines,

And our possessions,

Are either beautiful self-portraits, or loathsome mirrors that reflect the degree of our own fooling taking place.

>   This could be your last day on Earth.

>   What must be done today?

>   What do you instantly think about?

>   What do you need to do?

>   What do you need to say?

>   And to whom?

>   For whom?

>   With whom?

"Imagine that you are lying in an emergency room, critically injured, unable to speak or move, the concerned faces of loved ones floating above you, the pain beginning to dull from the morphine just injected. You wish to reach out to tell them something, to finish your business, to say good-by, to cut through years of partial communication.

What would you say? Think of what has remained unsaid and share that each day with those you love. Don't hesitate. Tomorrow is just a dream."

+ Stephen Levine, *Who Dies?*

WHAT DOES THINKING OF NOT THINKING LOOK LIKE?

41. My good friend, if you *think* you know what is going to happen to you within the next year,

Hour,

Minute,

Day,

Time,

Week,

Month,

And/or second,

Then please, my good friend, please think again.

Or, rather, please don't think in those measurements at all.

It'd be much simpler to follow the organic pattern of our spontaneous fate that effortlessly unfurls before our waterlogged optic-orbs every single day.

"There is a Taoist story of an old farmer who had worked his crops for many years. One day his horse ran away. Upon hearing the news, his neighbors came to visit. 'Such bad luck,' they said sympathetically. 'Maybe,' the farmer replied.

The next morning the horse returned, bringing with it three other wild horses. 'How wonderful,' the neighbors exclaimed. 'Maybe,' replied the old man.

The following day, his son tried to ride one of the untamed horses, was thrown, and broke his leg. The neighbors again came to offer their sympathy on his misfortune. 'Maybe,' answered the farmer.

The day after, military officials came to the village to draft young men into the army. Seeing that the son's leg was broken, they passed him by. The neighbors congratulated the farmer on how well things had turned out. 'Maybe,' said the farmer."

+ Unknown

KNOWING IS NOT KNOWING KNOWING
/
NOT KNOWING IS KNOWING NOT KNOWING
/
KNOWING IS KNOWING NOT KNOWING
/
NOT KNOWING IS NOT KNOWING KNOWING

42.

REFLEXIONS OF MIRARÉ

"The Net of Indra is a profound and subtle metaphor for the structure of reality. Imagine a vast net; at each crossing point there is a jewel, each jewel is perfectly clear and reflects all the other jewels in the net, the way two mirrors placed opposite each other will reflect an image ad infinitum."

+ Stephen Mitchell, *The Enlightened Mind*

43. Never once, upon any time, existed a sentient mirror with legs, a mouth, and a reflective glass.

    It lived in a humble hut somewhere in the desert and it didn't have an official name because well…it was a mirror.

    But for the sake of our interaction, it will be called:

    Mirror.

    And for repetition's sake it will also be called:

    It.

    As Mirror awoke on some obscure time and day, its first inclination was to head into Miraré.

    Mirror had never been to Miraré, let alone heard of it, until yesterday, by a truly breathtaking tale told by a local desert prophet.

The most interesting part of the tale, which impacted Mirror profoundly, was the oddity that Miraré people had never seen their reflection, and coincidentally, *neither had Mirror.*

Paradoxically, Mirror could reflect everything else but Itself. No bodies of water and no other reflective glasses were to be found anywhere near this desert.

But now, after years of strenuous searching for Its own reflection, Mirror knew that *this was it:* this was Its chance to finally see Itself.

As Mirror prepared to leave its humble abode, It stopped and reflected all of the objects in Its hut with a detached form of nostalgia. After a couple seconds of introspection, Mirror went on Its way, heading towards the first sand dune.

The first characters to materialize were two men in all-white lab coats.

One was holding a black-and-white spiraled notebook full of papers sticking out from every-which corner, while the other desperately clutched onto two glass beakers full of fizzy purple-ish liquid.

One of them ran up to Mirror, took out his pocket ruler, and started quantifying Mirror's dimensions in awe.

"Wow, what a specimen! What are you made of?" blurted out White Lab Coat #1.

Mirror responded: "Hello, good sirs, would you happen to know the way to Miraré?"

White Lab Coat #2 added, "*I* know exactly what this specimen *is* and what it's made of. *I* have perceived a similar specimen in the most recent, contemporary, up-to-date peer-reviewed journal!"

....

"Wellll….what did it say?" White Lab Coat #1 retorted indignantly.

"Oh right, it's uhhh…hmmm..let's dissect this specific case. I will—ummm—attempt to recover the memory by—ummm reconstructing a myriad of associations of whatever I recall about said peer-reviewed article—*that I have in fact read and understood*! Hmmm, ah yes, of course, I know now! This is a *mirorralis specificalus* and it is the resultant of an atom's nucleus that split itself open and organized itself into exactly 8 protons and 13 neutrons whose synapses in the post lateral region of the parietal lobe were la…"

Just as Mirror was going to repeat Its question about Miraré, the men continued their confusion elsewhere, walking further and further away.

Mirror continued on forward.

Trudging up the sand dune, secretly hoping to see Miraré from the peak and get this journey over with, Mirror encountered another man, a local preacher holding a small black book in his left hand, just before reaching the peak.

Mechanically, the preacher preached, "May the Good Lord bless you on this fine day gentle—hmmm…. You don't seem to be a man nor woman?….What kind of abomination are you!?"

"Look and you might see." replied Mirror, calmly pointing to his body—the reflective glass.

The preacher stole a glance from Mirror's glass and could not bear to see his reflection.

He readily snapped into a temper tantrum and increasingly turned tomato red with every other word he spewed forth, "I don't have time for these games with vermin like you! I already know what I look like! I already know who I am!"

Mirror replied: "Look, I don't have time for these games either buddy. Where can I find Miraré?"

The preacher ran away crying and Mirror continued on with indifference, sprinkled with some empathy for the confused little man.

The sweltering day floated onwards and Mirror's vision started blurring from the sandy winds beginning to pick up.

A pair of shrill voices simultaneously squawked: "AYE! CUM IN EYRE! SANDSTORMS A'STARTIN!"

Mirror ran towards what seemed like a melting igloo that somehow kept its form in the middle of the desert.

As Mirror stood there with sand and debris all over Its glass, the elderly couple's attitude turned hostile.

"Wha de hell areya supposedtah be?" they, again, croaked in unison.

"I'm –"

"Fuhget about it, looks lyke ya kneed a wipe," interjected the couple with a crude sort of harmony.

They somewhat cleaned Mirror's glass and distortedly saw themselves in the reflection.

The room's atmosphere immediately radiated an internal and external shift.

"Aye, so where yer goin tew?" they asked in a slightly subdued tone.

"Miraré. Do you know where it is?"

"Ah, dern't waste yer time. It dern't xsist."

"How do you know that?"

"We spernt our whole godderm lives chasin' that bullshit! and now we're stuck out her!" Go home."

In that instant, the whirligig of sand settled outside.

Mirror contemplated the words for some moments, thanked the couple, and promptly left the melting igloo.

Looking in all directions, not knowing which way was home and which way to Miraré,

Mirror picked a direction and sauntered on towards the next sand dune of seeming infinite grain.

As It reached the sandy summit's climax, Mirror's attention gravitated towards all directions, fervently searching for any trace and/or glimmer of Miraré, even though It had no idea what to look for exactly.

Everywhere looked the same.

Both frightened and excited as to where to turn, Mirror slid down the sand dune and dejectedly sauntered on to the next one.

After a couple minutes of ambling, Mirror saw a woman in a scarlet-checkered suit.

Her demeanor could be succinctly described as: walking at a brisk pace, with tightly hunched shoulders, a rigid frame, a calculator conveniently strapped inches away from her face (just enough so that she could barely see where she's stepping next), and a permanent facial expression of someone who just smelled a microwaved bag of shit.

She walked and walked and walked without taking any risks from taking her eyes off the numbers.

As the woman shouldered Mirror out of the way, It heard her mumble, "4 times 5 is 20, so if *I* sell, it could make…but wait, if *I* invest in that then it would be…okay then 4 x 6 is 24, square root it, multiply it by the power of 6, and *I* will profit approximately…545 koontash. Fuck! The margins will be compromised…I'm going to have to fire…"

Before Mirror could ask his now infamous question: "Where is Miraré?" the voice trailed off and continued its befuddlement elsewhere.

Tirelessly trotting up what seemed like the tallest sand dune around, Mirror encountered the village butcher.

He looked disheveled and out of breath, wearing nothing but a white apron and nothing underneath, while carrying a half-alive pheasant in his right hand.

Before the butcher could say anything, he saw himself in Mirror and gushed tears on impact.

"Why are you crying?" whispered Mirror as it tenderly cradled the butcher in Its arms.

The butcher, choking in tears, "I—I have personally hurt this animal, and many, many others back home. Who…—*Who am I!* to determine the course of their lives?" said the butcher as he took off his apron and now used it to nurture the pheasant back to life.

Mirror, avoiding to give overly-simplified philosophical advice to a complete stranger about his identity and moral framework, instead, interpreted this opportunity as a cue to ask Its now infamous question:"Soooo, excuse my timing sir, but I'm headed to Miraré. Am I going in the right direction?"

The butcher immediately perked up, slowly wiped the tears from his rosy cheeks, and began laughing like a madman.

He beamed Mirror with penetrating eyes, patted him on the back, and ran off with the in-recovery-pheasant.

Ready to turn back now, scared that It was venturing further and further away from home, Mirror resolved to climb this last sand dune and then figure it out from there.

As It now reached the apogee of what looked like the tallest sand dune in the nearest vicinity, again, a smiling face popped out from the top: "HAAALLOOH!"

Mirror stumbled backwards and fell on Its back.

The only thing Mirror now reflected was the boundless blue expanse and the flaming yellow disk blazing in the distantly near space.

A child's face, whose gargantuan hazel eyes screamed freedom, popped into the reflection, merging with the blue sky, and asked:

"Going to Miraré?!"

"Yes—yes, how'd you know? Am I almost there?"

The child's eyes continued radiating the Burning Cosmos with an accompanied smile blossoming on her petite countenance.

She bolted down the sand dune and Mirror followed.

As Mirror reached the bottom, It followed the child into a lazy river.

The child began washing Mirror's dusty glass and a nearby fly fisherman, along with the local desert wildlife, slowly gravitated towards them, overwhelming the surrounding riverbanks.

Lizards, camels, elephants, scorpions, fish, antelope, deer, lions, foxes, sheep, hares, baboons, jackals, hyenas, and such gathered around.

Mirror, standing in the lazy river with Its newly cleaned glass, reflected Itself to all those present with a shimmering clarity.

The fisherman, and the surrounding wildlife, ignoring their worldly duties, all stood in amazement before their purest reflections.

Mirror transformed the silence into an inquiry:

"Excuse me everyone, which way to Miraré?"

Speechless and smiling at their reflections, nobody could respond.

GETTING CLOSER TO WHAT IT SEEMS TO BE

> "…the only thing you have to offer to another human being, ever, is your own state of being."
>
> + Ram Dass, *The Only Dance There Is*

44. To write is to attempt to make sense of thought.

    To attempt to make sense of thought is to attempt to make sense of suffering.

    And to attempt to make sense of suffering is to attempt to make sense of Life.

    Keyword: *attempt*.

    All I seem to be is an indifferent movement of sentient light-energy writing down what makes sense to my individual experience so far.

    I am not trying to save you, enlighten you, nor teach you anything new.

    Mostly because all of those are impossible to do, but also because those things would only serve to pacify, numb, and distract you from searching for your own Truth, *if it even exists at all*.

"Now we can never know *all* the forms of Truth—psychological truth, sociological truth, economic truth, biological truth, and so on. These forms ceaselessly advance and evolve, alter and complexify. And although we can never know all these forms of Truth, we can know Truth itself, or the absolute reality of which all these forms are but partial and approximate reflections. In other words, although we can never know all the facts of existence, we can know the Fact of Existence which underlies and grounds all possible and relative facts, just as, once we know the ocean is wet, we know all waves are wet, even though we may never know each and every wave."

+ Ken Wilber, *The Simple Feeling of Being*

EXISTENCE ATTEMPTING TO EXPLAIN EXISTENCE

45. The ultimate irony of Existence is Existence attempting to explain Existence.

"There is no greater mystery than this, that we keep seeking reality though in fact we are reality. We think there is something hiding reality and that this must be destroyed before reality is gained. How ridiculous!"

+ Ramana Maharshi

THE FLAME FLICKERS

46. A vermillion candle whose sole existence was made for this moment, and only for this moment, merges its unstable light to the sensuous aroma of this intentionally dark room.

> *The flame flickers.*

An obscure guitar materializes from an iPhone's steely mouth.

> *The flame flickers.*

Who am I?

> *The flame flickers.*

Who are you?

> *The flame flickers.*

What is all of *this*?

> *The flame flickers.*

Where are we traveling to?

> *The flame flickers.*

Let's party.

> *The flame flickers.*

Using present time to speak of future time.

The flame flickers.

Are we enjoying what needs to be enjoyed in this Lifetime?

The flame flickers.

Are we learning what needs to be learned in this Lifetime?

The flame flickers.

Is there anything to be *truly learned*?

The flame flickers.

Where does Peace lie?

The flame flickers.

Where will The Truth come through next?

The flame flickers.

Welcome to the Shape of Forms where we all Shape our Forms with Shaping.

The flame flickers.

We all play with Forms within The Form.

The flame flickers.

And also with the Forms within the Forms within The Form.

The flame flickers.

Subconscious desires firing at justifiable speeds of forgiveness.

The flame flickers.

Let's all be fully enlightened right now!

The flame flickers.

Ready:

The flame flickers.

4...

3...

2...

1...

0...

-1...

-2....

-3....

-4....

0....

The flame flickers.

Desire.

Allow.

Desire.

Allow.

Desire.

Reject.

Desire.

Reject.

> *The flame flickers.*

What is there to ultimately protect?

> *The flame flickers.*

Open sesame.

> *The flame flickers.*

Note to My Self:

The flame flickers.

FULFILLMENT

47. Man cannot live without desires, as is sometimes misinterpreted and believed to be so.

    The inherent nature and design of our Basic Being includes desire:

    Eating, shelter, comfort, and connection.

    This belief of "eradicating desire" seems to have innocently originated in our Collective Memory, predominantly through Eastern thought, and subsequently pilfered down by Buddha's gentle admonitions of eradicating desire as the secret to overcome suffering.

    The reason, it seems, for the teaching of a complete eradication of desires is this:

    For one to come closer to the illuminating discovery that almost all of one's previous desires were never chosen by the highest portion of one's intelligence.

    That almost all of one's previous desires have been obliviously hand-picked by their: untested assumptions, by their self-centered conditionings, by their tedious prejudices, and finally, by unknown influences that one has unknowingly carried around their neck like a fifty-pound barbell for years on end.

    It seems that once this illuminating discovery is made, and dually, sincerely acknowledged, a new form of clarity makes itself known, and, subsequently, leads one to then freely follow new desires one consciously chooses, as opposed to being pulled like an invisible magnet to those paltry, substance-less desires in which one was unfortunately unaware of before.

This clarity is akin to the immediate understanding that one was previously dreaming without the conscious knowing that they were dreaming.

Complete fulfillment will, and can never be completely fulfilled.

How can we reasonably think that complete fulfillment exists in this Existence?

Our inherent drive for anything would cease entirely.

What would that do to human evolution?

What would that do to human civilization?

What would that do to our individual existences?

That would stop all of our seeking, our searching, our desiring, our progress toward higher and more transcendent ways of being and living.

Yet, despite all of this, we will still, somehow, never tire of asking the answerless question:

Where is true fulfillment and happiness to be found in this Life?

"Thus, in the world of Form, the ultimate Omega appears as an ever-receding horizon of fulfillment (the ever-receding horizon of the totality of manifestation), forever pulling us forward, forever retreating itself, thus always conferring wholeness and partialness in the same breath: the wholeness of this moment is part of the whole of the next moment: the world is always complete and incomplete in any given moment, and thus condemned to a fulfillment that is never fulfilled: the forms rush and run forward to a reward that retreats with the run itself."

+ Ken Wilber, *The Simple Feeling of Being*

FRIENDS

"Of all things beyond my power, I value nothing more than a friendship with people who sincerely love the truth."

+ Baruch Spinoza

48. Any activity that includes friends, laughter, sincerity, and lightheartedness,

All in one,

Is good and worth pursuing.

"For, in truth, there is no "other." There is just being, experienced from different focal points. When you are fully present, you see there is no such thing as "another person." There are just two perceptions of the one existence. There is "your" unfolding and there's "mine." Our work is to come together in truth. To become the perfect environment for each other's recognition that there is no other, but just the One to be shared."

+ Stephen Levine, *Who Dies?*

ART, MEMORY, & JUNG'S COLLECTIVE UNCONSCIOUS

49. Found in James McConkey's anthology: *The Anatomy of Memory*, Jung's essay "Psychology and Literature" seeks to explain literature's role in shaping memory. And although Jung principally focuses on psychology and literature, one begins to quickly see that he also integrates his view on art's role in shaping memory as well.

Jung begins by outlining artistic creation as belonging to either of two modes: *psychological* or *visionary*. He uses both modes to construct his argument and relates them to: creativity, the collective unconscious, and memory. Throughout the excerpt though, one begins to quickly intuit Jung's preference for the visionary mode of creation as opposed to the psychological, while delineating both of their merits and both of their shortcomings.

Let us start by defining Jung's interpretation of the *psychological* mode of artistic creation:

"The *psychological* mode deals with materials drawn from the realm of human consciousness—for instance, with the lessons of life, with emotional shocks, the experience of passion and the crises of human destiny in general—all of which go to make up the conscious life of man, and his feeling life in particular" (150).

Jung proceeds to claim that the *psychological* is the mode artists predominantly utilize whose "work is an interpretation and illumination of the contents of consciousness, of the ineluctable experiences of human life with its eternally recurrent sorrow and joy" (150). Through these *psychological* creations, an artist is able to show the insights they have gleaned through their own life and then relate it to others who either choose to evade, or ignore aspects of human consciousness: suffering, grief, anxiety, ego, identity, faith, etc.

In terms of its limitations, according to Jung, "Whatever its particular form may be, the psychological work of art always takes its materials from the vast realm of conscious human experience—from the vivid foreground of life, we might say. I have called this mode of artistic creation psychological because in its activity it nowhere transcends the bounds of psychological intelligibility" (151). This is a major problem in Jung's perspective because it does not account for what transcends reason, logic, and does not penetrate deep enough into the memories stored in the recesses of our minds—*the collective unconscious.*

This is where the *visionary* mode of artistic creation enters: "It is a strange something that derives its existence from the hinterland of man's mind—that suggests the abyss of time separating us from pre-human ages, or evokes a super-human world of contrasting light and darkness. It is a primordial experience which surpasses man's understanding" (151). This is an artistic mode that Jung truly believes shapes the bulk of humanity's memory and how we view the world, using ancient memory that "arises from timeless depths," and the artist as its vehicle.

The main rift between both the psychological and the visionary mode of creation is what it evokes from individuals. On one side, the *psychological* is one in which the material is fairly intelligible and able to be explained; it is direct and tells you what the message is. As opposed to the *visionary* in which one is either "…astonished, taken aback, confused, put on our guard or even disgusted—and we demand commentaries and explanations. We are reminded in nothing of everyday, human life, but rather of dreams, nighttime fears and the dark recesses of the mind that we sometimes sense with misgiving" (152). With the *visionary*, the artist and viewer are invited to partially glimpse into our collective unconscious which Jung defines as: "…a certain psychic disposition shaped by the forces of heredity; from it consciousness has developed" (157).

In other words, the collective unconscious is a shared memory-complex between members of a species (or of all species together) which includes certain archetypes, information, and behaviors. He believes that some poets, seers, mystics, and artists are the ones who are able to bore a hole into the veil of ignorance and access this database of memories supposedly available to us all. This database is "not wholly unfamiliar. Man has known of it from time immemorial" (156).

Why are most of us unaware of this database? Jung says that it is due to a "fear of superstition and metaphysics, and because we strive to construct a conscious world that is safe and manageable in that natural law holds in it the place of statute law in a commonwealth" (156).

Jung believes that this collective unconscious is within and accessible by everyone, yet it is usually the "…poet, a seer or a leader [that] allows himself to be guided by the unexpressed desire of his times and shows the way, by word or deed, to the attainment of that which everyone blindly craves and expects —whether this attainment results in good or evil, the healing of an epoch or its destruction" (158).

And how does the collective unconscious manifest through the poet, artist, seer, and/or leader?

Creativity.

And where does creativity come from?

Jung answers this question with another question, "What if there were some living force whose sphere of action lies beyond our world of every day" (155)?

It seems that Jung is implying that there is a *force far greater than ourselves* which regularly manifests itself in the poet, artist, and/or mystic through creativity. This creativity is then used to create some form of art that does not come from the artist's personal will but is "moulded by the unconscious" where the "conscious ego is swept along on a subterranean current, being nothing more than a helpless observer of events. The work in process becomes the poet's fate and determines his psychic development" (161).

Essentially, the artist is a vessel for an intelligent, sentient force to pour itself through and create something marvelous and/or repulsive. This intelligent, sentient force is so large and inspiriting, that it not only fills oneself, but spills over into others as well, simultaneously shaping one's current era and its variegated dynamics. Each period, according to Jung, has its own "limitations of conscious outlook" and "requires a compensatory adjustment" which is regulated through the collective unconscious—the repository of mankind's memories.

Jung explains a "primordial experience" which manifests through the visionary artist "…like a whirlwind that seizes everything within reach and, by carrying it aloft, assumes a visible shape. [And] Since the particular expression can never exhaust the possibilities of the vision…the poet must have at his disposal a huge store of materials if he is to communicate even a few of his intimations" (157).

This "primordial experience" Jung describes, sounds familiar to typical near-death, religious, and drug-related experiences in which one's "normal" state of consciousness is altered showing one certain insights, visions, and opportunities to explore Consciousness from never-before-seen-angles. He uses Dante, Goethe, Blake, and Nietzsche as exemplars of visionary artistry. These men, to Jung, have served as instruments for this intelligent, sentient force to flow through which does not reflect their total will, nor self at all. Nor are they expected to interpret anything.

"A great work of art is like a dream; for all its apparent obviousness it does not explain itself and is never unequivocal. A dream never says: 'You ought,' or: 'This is the truth.' It presents an image in much the same way as nature allows a plant to grow, and we must draw our own conclusions" (162).

In a similar context, we must draw our own conclusions with visionary art and cast aside the details of the artist's personal lives which should not affect one's view of their art. We must be able to view a piece of art with as little preconceptions as possible and let the illuminating energy that was poured into the artist similarly pour into us. We see that the artist "…has drawn upon the healing and redeeming forces of the collective psyche that underlies consciousness . . . he has penetrated to that matrix of life in which all men are embedded, which imparts a common rhythm to all human existence, and allows the individual to communicate his feeling and his striving to mankind as a whole" (162). This is what Jung believes that visionary art is able to accomplish that psychological art can only hope to evolve to someday.

* * *

Existence, to Jung, is all interfused, in which memory is not exempt. In a similar vein, James McConkey opines and adds to Jung's philosophy in his abstract: "Perspectives of Memory," with the notion of a collective unconscious: "…not only does the past inform the present, but the present informs the past. In other words, the understanding of our present selves that memory provides us is capable of returning the gift, enabling us to know our earlier selves in a manner that eluded us then" (311). With past memories informing our present self, we are able to make wiser decisions in how we view and interact with life in the future.

In another abstract, McConkey connects the unconscious "to our beginning within the natural world, to our genetic memories; it represents that . . . spiritual part which links all of humanity." McConkey and Jung agree that the unconscious "is a component of our dream world . . . essential to inspiration and creativity . . . and a vast category into which we put all that remains mysterious about our responses and behavior, all that eludes rationality" (447).

Simply, the collective unconscious is completely irrational and mysterious.

In this irrationality lies a potential justification for why most people, living in a reason-dominated world, have lost the ability and courage to activate this aspect of one's inner world. According to Jung, "There has never been a primitive culture that did not possess a system of secret teaching. . . . The men's councils and the totem-clans preserve this teaching about hidden things that lie apart from man's daytime existence—things which, from primeval times, have always constituted his most vital experiences" (156). This explains the mystery schools in ancient Greece and the secret societies that still run behind the scenes today. The "secrets" in these institutions are relayed to those who will hopefully retain this knowledge and one day impart it to those within their own tribe, and so on.

With all of this in mind, Jung's seemingly rhetorical question feels timely, "Do we delude ourselves in thinking that we possess and command our own souls" (155)?

Do we truly believe that we fully and consciously shape our own individual memory? which in turn shapes the collective memory?

Jung believes it is through this chain from a *higher, creative living force*—to the artist—to the viewer—and back to this *higher, creative living force* in which memory is shaped. We are dealing with a *living force* that is co-creating our memories and using art as its primary vehicle to influence both our collective and individual past, present, and future memory-complex.

It is through the artist, the poet, and the mystic, that this *higher, creative living force* perpetually manifests itself and shows us that Life will always be more mysterious than we previously thought it to be.

A PERPETUAL PAINTING OF MEANING

"How can you expect an onlooker to live a picture of mine as I lived it? A picture comes to me from miles away: who is to say from how far away I sensed it, saw it, painted it; and yet the next day I can't see what I've done myself. How can anyone enter into my dreams, my instincts, my desires, my thoughts, which have taken a long time to mature and to come out into the daylight, and above all grasp from them what I have been about—perhaps against my own will."

+ Pablo Picasso, *Picasso: In His Words*

50. In one of its most vivid interpretations, one could say that:

    Creating any work of Art is one of the highest mediums we currently possess of *painting meaning onto the canvas of our perceptual landscape.*

    And since the degrees of meaning we perpetually ascribe to things within our perception is the most meaningful thing we can do in this Lifetime,

    We must continuously start over and begin once again.

SHARING EXCITEMENT

51. Why are we immediately compelled to share something with others when we're truly excited about something important to us?

"And therefore, all of those for whom authentic transformation deeply unseated their souls must, I believe, wrestle with the profound moral obligation to shout from the heart—perhaps quietly and gently, with tears of reluctance; perhaps with fierce fire and angry wisdom; perhaps with slow and careful analysis; perhaps by unshakable public example—but *authenticity* always and absolutely carries a *demand* and *duty:* you must speak out, to the best of your ability, and shake the spiritual tree, and shine your headlights into the eyes of the complacent. You must let that radical realization rumble through your veins and rattle those around you.

Alas, if you fail to do so, you are betraying your own authenticity. You are hiding your true estate. You don't want to upset others because you don't want to upset yourself. You are acting in bad faith, the taste of a bad infinity.

Because, you see, the alarming fact is that any realization of depth carries a terrible burden: Those who are allowed to see are simultaneously saddled with the obligation to *communicate* that vision in no uncertain terms: that is the bargain. You were allowed to see the truth under the agreement that you would communicate it to others (that is the ultimate meaning of the bodhisattva vow). And therefore, if you have seen, you simply must speak out."

+ Ken Wilber, *One Taste*

○

52. Truth is the greatest dream within this Great Dream.

DEDICATION

To:

       Existence

BIBLIOGRAPHY

Kerouac, Jack, and Todd F. Tietchen. *Visions of Cody*. Library of America 2015.

Schopenhauer, Arthur. *Essays and Aphorisms*. Translated by R.J Hollingdale, Penguin, 2004.

Wilber, Ken. *The Simple Feeling of Being: Embracing Your True Nature*. Edited by Mark Palmer, Sean Hargens, Vipassana Esbjörn, and Adam Leonard. Shambhala, 2004.

PART ONE

Seneca, Lucius Annaeus. *Letters from a Stoic*. Translated by Robin Campbell, Penguin Classics, 2014.

THE INTRODUCTION TO THE CONCLUSION

Camus, Albert. *The Myth of Sisyphus*. Translated by Justin O'Brien, Vintage International, 1991.

Pessoa, Fernando. *The Book of Disquiet*. Ed. & trans. by Richard Zenith, Penguin Classics, 2015.

FRACTAL ONE

Whitman, Walt. *Song of Myself*. Edited by Stephen Mitchell, Shambhala, 1998.

FRACTAL TWO

Pater, Walter. *Studies in the History of the Renaissance*. Edited by Matthew Beaumont, Oxford University Press, 2010.

FRACTAL THREE

Osho. *This Very Body the Buddha*. Jaico Publishing House, 2006.

Caputi, Anthony. *Eight Modern Plays: The Wild Duck, Three Sisters, Candida, the Ghost Sonata, Six Characters in Search of an Author, Long Day's Journey into Night, Mother Courage and Her Children, Happy Days: Backgrounds and Criticism*. W.W. Norton, 1991.

FRACTAL FOUR

Reps, Paul. *Zen Flesh, Zen Bones: A Collection of Zen and Pre-Zen Writings*. Tuttle Publishing, 1998.

Aurelius, Marcus. *Meditations*. Edited by Martin Hammond, Penguin Classics, 2014.

Wilber, Ken. *The Essential Ken Wilber*. Shambhala, 1998.

Wilber, Ken. *The Essential Ken Wilber*. Shambhala, 1998.

FRACTAL FIVE

Levine, Stephen. *Who Dies?: An Investigation of Conscious Living and Conscious Dying*. Gateway, 2001.

Camus, Albert. *The Myth of Sisyphus*. Translated by Justin O'Brien, Vintage International, 1991.

Camus, Albert. *The Myth of Sisyphus*. Translated by Justin O'Brien, Vintage International, 1991.

Voltaire. *Candide*. Translated by Lowell Bair, Bantam Dell, 2003.

Kübler-Ross Elisabeth. "Death Does Not Exist." *On Life after Death*. Celestial Arts, 2008.

FRACTAL SIX

Seneca, Lucius Annaeus. *Letters from a Stoic*. Translated by Robin Campbell, Penguin Classics, 2014.

FRACTAL SEVEN

Pessoa, Fernando. *The Book of Disquiet*. Ed. & trans. by Richard Zenith, Penguin Classics, 2015.

FRACTAL EIGHT

Tzu, Lao. *Hua Hu Ching: the Unknown Teachings of Lao Tzu*. Translated by Brian Browne Walker, HarperCollins, 2009.

FRACTAL NINE

Seneca, Lucius Annaeus. *Letters from a Stoic*. Translated by Robin Campbell, Penguin Classics, 2014.

Von Goethe, Johann Wolfgang. *Goethe's Faust*. Translated by Walter Kaufmann, Anchor, 1962.

Nachmanovitch, Stephen. *Free Play: Improvisation in Life and Art*. G.P. Putnam's Sons, 1991.

FRACTAL TEN

Sartre, Jean-Paul. *No Exit and Three Other Plays*. Translated by Stuart Gilbert, Vintage, 1989.

Mitchell, Stephen, translator. *Gilgamesh: A New English Version*. Atria Books, 2006.

FRACTAL ELEVEN

Schopenhauer, Arthur. *Essays and Aphorisms*. Translated by R.J Hollingdale, Penguin, 2004.

Schopenhauer, Arthur. *Essays and Aphorisms*. Translated by R.J Hollingdale, Penguin, 2004.

Pessoa, Fernando. *The Book of Disquiet*. Ed. & trans. by Richard Zenith, Penguin Classics, 2015.

FRACTAL TWELVE

Schopenhauer, Arthur. *Essays and Aphorisms*. Translated by R.J Hollingdale, Penguin, 2004.

Aurelius, Marcus. *Meditations*. Edited by Martin Hammond, Penguin Classics, 2014.

CONCLUDING INTRODUCTIONS

Schopenhauer, Arthur. *Essays and Aphorisms*. Translated by R.J Hollingdale, Penguin, 2004.

Spira, Rupert. "The Daily Quote from Rupert Spira." *Rupert Spira: Contemplating the Nature of Experience*, 15 July 2018.

PART DEUX

1. Wilde, Oscar. *De Profundis and Other Prison Writings*. Edited by Colm Toibin, Penguin Classics, 2013.

2. Spira, Rupert. *The Transparency of Things: Contemplating the Nature of Experience*. Sahaja, 2016.

3. Wilber, Ken. *The Simple Feeling of Being: Embracing Your True Nature*. Edited by Mark Palmer, Sean Hargens, Vipassana Esbjörn, and Adam Leonard. Shambhala, 2004.

4. Krishnamurti, Jiddu. *Freedom from the Known*. Harper Collins, 1975.

Picasso, Pablo. *Picasso: In His Words*. Edited by Hiro Clark, Collins Publication San Francisco, 1993.

5. Rimbaud, Arthur. *Arthur Rimbaud: Complete Works*. Edited by Paul Schmidt, Harper Perennial Modern Classics, 2008.

   Wilber, Ken. *The Simple Feeling of Being: Embracing Your True Nature*. Edited by Mark Palmer, Sean Hargens, Vipassana Esbjörn, and Adam Leonard. Shambhala, 2004.

   Hegel, Georg Wilhelm Friedrich. "Logic." *The European Philosophers from Descartes to Nietzsche*, edited by Monroe C. Beardsley, Modern Library, 2002.

   Pessoa, Fernando. *The Book of Disquiet*. Ed. & trans. by Richard Zenith, Penguin Classics, 2015.

   Harris, Sam. *Waking Up: A Guide to Spirituality Without Religion*. Simon & Schuster, 2015.

6. Parmenides. *On Nature*. Translated by Thomas Davidson, trisagionseraph.tripod.com/Texts/Poem.html.

   Tzu, Lao. *Tao Teh Ching*. Translated by John C. H. Wu, Shambhala Publications Inc, 2006.

7. Harris, Sam. *Waking Up: A Guide to Spirituality Without Religion*. Simon & Schuster, 2015.

8. Baym, Nina, et al., editors. *The Norton Anthology of American Literature*. 8th ed., B, W. W. Norton & Company, 2011.

9. Emerson, Ralph Waldo. *Ralph Waldo Emerson: Selected Journals 1820-1842*. Edited by Lawrence Rosenwald, vol. 1, Library of America, 2010.

10. Maharshi, Ramana, and David Godman. *Be As You Are: The Teachings of Sri Ramana Maharshi*. Arkana (Penguin Books), 1985.

11. Wilde, Oscar. *De Profundis and Other Prison Writings*. Edited by Colm Toibin, Penguin Classics, 2013.

    Schopenhauer, Arthur. *Essays and Aphorisms*. Translated by R.J Hollingdale, Penguin, 2004.

    Suzuki, Shunryu. *Zen Mind, Beginner's Mind: Informal Talks on Zen Meditation and Practice*. Edited by Trudy Dixon, Weatherhill, 2000.

12. Pater, Walter. *Marius the Epicurean: His Sensations and Ideas*. Cosimo Classics, 2005.

    Krishnamurti, Jiddu. *Freedom from the Known*. Harper Collins, 1975.

13. Harris, Sam. *Waking Up: A Guide to Spirituality Without Religion*. Simon & Schuster, 2015.

15. Padmasambhava. *The Tibetan Book of the Dead: First Complete Translation* . Edited by Graham Coleman and Thupten Jinpa. Translated by Gyurme Dorje, Penguin Classics, 2007.

16. Edman, Irwin. *Arts and the Man: A Short Introduction to Aesthetics*. W. W. Norton & Company, 1960.

17. Rilke, Rainer Maria. *Letters to a Young Poet*. Merchant Books, 2012.

18. Montaigne, Michel de. "On the Education of Children." *Montaigne: Essays*. Edited by John M. Cohen, Penguin Books, 1993.

    Pater, Walter. *Studies in the History of the Renaissance*. Edited by Matthew Beaumont, Oxford University Press, 2010.

19. Kaplan, Charles, and William Davis Anderson, editors. *Criticism: Major Statements*. 4th ed., Bedford/St. Martin's, 1999.

20. Pessoa, Fernando. *The Book of Disquiet*. Ed. & trans. by Richard Zenith, Penguin Classics, 2015.

> Osho. *Fame, Fortune, and Ambition: What Is the Real Meaning of Success?* St. Martin's Griffin, 2010.

21. Harari, Yuval Noah. *Sapiens: A Brief History of Humankind*. 1st ed., Harper, 2015.

22. Schopenhauer, Arthur. *Essays and Aphorisms*. Translated by R.J Hollingdale, Penguin, 2004.

23. Robb, Graham. *Balzac: A Life*. W. W. Norton & Co Inc, 1994.

25. Krishnamurti, Jiddu. *Think on These Things*. Edited by D. Rajagopal, HarperOne, 1989.

> Botton, Alain de. *The Consolations of Philosophy*, Pantheon Books, New York, 2000.

> Montaigne, Michel de. *The Complete Essays*. Edited by M. A. Screech, London, Penguin Classics, 1991.

26. Levine, Stephen. *Who Dies?: An Investigation of Conscious Living and Conscious Dying*. Gateway, 2001.

> Seneca, Lucius Annaeus. *Letters from a Stoic*. Translated by Robin Campbell, Penguin Classics, 2014.

27. Harris, Sam. *Waking Up: A Guide to Spirituality Without Religion*. Simon & Schuster, 2015.

> Rimbaud, Arthur. *Illuminations*. Edited by Louise Varèse, New Directions, 1957.

29. Watson, Burton. *The Complete Works of Chuang Tzu*. Columbia University Press, 1968.

    Kundera, Milan. *The Art of the Novel*. Translated by Linda Asher, Harper Perennial, 2006.

30. Osho. T*he Art of Living and Dying*, Watkins Publishing, 2013.

31. Gibran, Khalil. *A Third Treasury of Kahlil Gibran*. Edited by Andrew Dib Sherfan, Castle Books, 1979.

    Krishnamurti, Jiddu. *Freedom from the Known*. Harper Collins, 1975.

    Voltaire. *Candide*. Translated by Lowell Bair, Bantam Dell, 2003.

    Camus, Albert. *The Myth of Sisyphus*. Translated by Justin O'Brien, Vintage International, 1991.

32. Merton, Thomas. *Zen and the Birds of Appetite*. New Directions, 1968.

33. Po, Huang. *The Zen Teaching of Huang Po: On the Transmission of Mind*. Edited by John Blofeld, Grove Press, 1994.

34. Russell, Bertrand. *The Problems of Philosophy*. Oxford University Press, 1997.

    Seneca, Lucius Annaeus. *Letters from a Stoic*. Translated by Robin Campbell, Penguin Classics, 2014.

35. Montaigne, Michel de. "On Experience." *Montaigne: Essays*. Edited by John M. Cohen, Penguin Books, 1993.

37. Montaigne, Michel de. "On the Education of Children." *Montaigne: Essays*. Edited by John M. Cohen, Penguin Books, 1993.

38. Currey, Mason, editor. *Daily Rituals: How Artists Work*. Knopf, 2013.

40. Levine, Stephen. *Who Dies?: An Investigation of Conscious Living and Conscious Dying*. Gateway, 2001.

41. "Maybe." Photographic Psychology: Interpreting People Pics, truecenterpublishing.com/zenstory/maybe.html.

43. Mitchell, Stephen, editor. *The Enlightened Mind*. Harper Perennial 1993.

44. Dass, Ram. *The Only Dance There Is: Talks at the Menninger Foundation, 1970, and Spring Grove Hospital, 1972* . Anchor, 1974.

   Wilber, Ken. *The Simple Feeling of Being: Embracing Your True Nature*. Edited by Mark Palmer, Sean Hargens, Vipassana Esbjörn, and Adam Leonard. Shambhala, 2004.

45. Mitchell, Stephen, editor. *The Enlightened Mind*. Harper Perennial 1993.

47. Wilber, Ken. *The Simple Feeling of Being: Embracing Your True Nature*. Edited by Mark Palmer, Sean Hargens, Vipassana Esbjörn, and Adam Leonard. Shambhala, 2004.

48. Mitchell, Stephen, editor. *The Enlightened Mind*. Harper Perennial 1993.

   Levine, Stephen. *Who Dies?: An Investigation of Conscious Living and Conscious Dying*. Gateway, 2001.

49. McConkey, James. *The Anatomy of Memory: An Anthology*. Oxford University Press, 1996.

50. Picasso, Pablo. *Picasso: In His Words*. Edited by Hiro Clark, Collins Publication San Francisco, 1993.

51. Wilber, Ken. *One Taste: Daily Reflections on Integral Spirituality*. Shambhala, 2000.

Copyright © 2019 Sebastian Rozo

Cover design by Stephen Rozo

The Awakened Moment

Stamford, CT

All rights reserved.

ISBN-13: 978-0-578-46658-3

ISBN-10: ISBN-10: 0-578-46658-9

Also by Sebastian:

As It Is

To Know Is To Know That You Don't Know

www.sebrozo.com

www.ingramcontent.com/pod-product-compliance
Lightning Source LLC
Chambersburg PA
CBHW022354040426
42450CB00005B/171